# Soaring with Angels

August 29, 2012

Dear Ngozi,

I cherish your friendship.

Shams Tabriz

# Soaring with Angels

shams-tabriz

**rumi**
HOUSE

Copyright 2011 ©

All rights reserved.

ISBN-13: 978-0-9878910-0-6

# DEDICATION

To that blessed pulse within us all…

# Awakening to Brilliance

This is the story of my life. Not my whole life, but the verses that have been relevant to my divine discovery of self.

This is the story of a seeker peeling away at the layers of his self to reveal a raw and naked beauty more brilliant than his eyes had ever seen. The story of the wretched finding his nobility. Of a friend who is both a teacher and his student, both a master and his pupil.

This is the story of a man discovering his divinity. Not simply becoming aware that he is a spark of the divine, but experiencing what it is to *be* divine. Embracing all the seemingly fragmented expressions of self and uniting them in an incredible experience of wholeness. Connecting his expanded consciousness to the universal consciousness that embraces all that is.

This is the story of a man soaring with angels. Releasing notions of separation and distinction from that angelic realm of grace and wisdom. Expanding his sense of self into that of the angelic realm. Inviting that realm to find expression within his being and within his world.

This is the story of foolishness. This is the story of bravery. This is the story of paradoxes. This is a fairy tale made real—a frog made prince through a number of kisses that revealed himself to himself.

This is my story. And I offer it to you with all the humility I can express. Not the humility of convention that simply deludes us into self diminishment, but the true humility that renders a state of awe and wonder at the discovery of the magnificence of oneself and others. I share with you my experiences at shedding my many layers of discombobulation to reveal to you what I revealed to myself.

I share with you my story so that you may know that beneath the veneer of your own selfish insignificance is a brilliance so divine that it simply must be revealed and freed to express. It is you. And it is me!

Laugh with me as you read this for I have played the fool. I have cried and I have doubted. I have fumed and I have judged. But today's fool seasoned by my awesome discovery is much the innocent child entering heaven. He is much the angel expressing as man.

Today I am very much the one urging his friend on. Be my friend.

# *Awareness*

You may wonder, who am I to say I am divine?

I have no explanation for those who do not accept the possibility of their divinity. For that, in truth, is the first step in self-discovery. Awareness. Accepting that one is divine by one's very nature—and accepting that one may come to consciously know and live their divinity.

If not for this first and most fundamental premise, *Awareness*, one cannot proceed to discover their truth. It would be an act of futility, an exercise of the uninspired intellect, an egoic fantasy.

So for those who do not at this moment accept this possibility, I say, *believe!*

Sufi tradition refers to the experience of self realization as *fanafillah*. Appropriately translated, this means the annihilation of self into God. I have experienced this as a complete dissolution of self—all notions of individuality and self-identification—and a resultant merging into the most magnificent and sublime nature of the source.

Such experiences have been spoken of by many mystics from many traditions. And each describes it differently according to their own understanding and ability—or willingness—to translate the experience.

I have enjoyed levels of this experience that include an overwhelming energetic expansion of my being in which my sense of self is lost and I find myself resonating with the universal rhythm that is the pulse of all that is. It is truly a mind-altering experience.

At other times I have dipped so deeply into silence that I find myself in a stillness completely devoid of any thing or any thought, while at the same time profoundly knit in a most sublime love.

This is the experience of touching the very core of my being. That element that is intimately connected with the source of all that is. That experiences no separation from all that is. That in essence *is* all that is.

There is another state of self-knowing that is the promise to humanity. This has been my journey and this is the subject of my story. *Divine human experience.*

It can be accurately described as *being* the angel in human form. Bringing the immensity of wonder and awe and wisdom and love that is the state of the angelic realm into the experience of a living, breathing, creative human being. It is this discovery of the divine birthright of us all, which is the natural transformational process that is upon us.

We stand in a unique moment in the evolution of mankind. The floodgates are open. God is shining upon us. And the discovery of our divinity is available for us to embrace. It is not that all of mankind will embrace this truth now, but many will. There is much in the realm of the unseen that greatly supports such an expansion.

This discovery that I speak of is the true understanding of our divine humanity. It is the healing of the self. The realignment of the self. The emergence of the healthy ego.

It is humanity walking individually and collectively with the full knowing of their own magnificence and the equivalent grandeur of all. It is the experience of wholeness and of sameness. The expression of compassion and love. Of creativity. It is our inheritance. And it is upon us.

And so it has been my humble, awesome experience to discover my divinity. The process has been often profound and often uncomfortable. It has brought up much in my emotional and physical memory that required forgiveness and compassion —and letting go.

It has called for patience and persistence. It has required faith. It has led to self examination. It has taught me the great magic of laughter and of playing the fool. It has expanded my understanding of me and of all of humanity.

It has brought me love in forms that were unimaginable. And it has inspired me to express that love.

Today, I can honor the efforts of the nestled caterpillar awakened to her evolution. Awakened to the brilliance of the fragrant world awaiting. Aware of the winged angel-worm destiny that beckons. The course is set. It is only for us to break free of our cocoons. To discard the notions of old, the judgments of old, the feelings of old, the patterns of old. The things that no longer enrich us. That no longer align our identity with the divine identity that is our truth.

Discovering divinity is eternal. For divinity is forever expansive, forever in creation. Know, however, that the point of recognizing your divinity, honoring your divinity, embracing it and being it is a significant moment in time. It is a grand, grand accomplishment. Strive for this. Desire it. And know that it is real.

For I shall be asking you, *Who are you to say that you are* not *divine?*

# Elmarilla

A great plan had been hatched to set upon this stage a common man with a common life. And this life was carefully crafted to accent the hurdles mankind comes to face in coming to know themselves.

Ah, but a secret was held, unknown even to him. This man had been seeded with a hidden impulse to seek the divine! That craving had been embedded times before into his subtle knowing. And so as he lived, seeking this knowledge arose as his deepest compulsion.

When this man was still young, a series of planned events unfolded in his life. They shook his foundations and caused him to question everything. A short time later and on the other side of his great land he encountered a very wise woman. She, too, had been set upon this stage with purpose.

This gentle lady was amazing. She knew of things our man had only dreamed to fathom. She spoke with a great surety, spoke of things that stoked the flames of curiosity that burned within him. This lady was a giant.

For much of her life this woman was the voice of celestial wisdom from a realm intimately and compassionately connected to the divine evolution of the human experience. She taught many people of their unique magnificence and the truth of their divinity.

This woman embraced life to lend her energies to the changing dynamic of humankind. She came to remind those with ears to hear of their divine birthright—and to awaken the ready seeds of divinity which lay dormant on the stage.

Slowly, patiently, with great love and compassion and with tremendous vision, our lady reminded the young man who he truly was. She reminded him of his true self and urged him to discover his purpose in being.

As he expanded, she revealed more of herself to him in order to further reflect to him the truth of who he was. She expressed as a mother to him. And this fine man understood.

Slowly and steadfastly he set aside his disbelief and doubt and embraced the possibility of magnificence. He discovered much that served to define the mold he was to fill in this life. He embraced his role as protector. He embraced his role as herald.

He embraced his role as a man discovering the fullness of his divinity. As teacher. As seeker. As lover. As way-shower. As friend.

When this man had witnessed enough of his beauty to ensure a continued expansion into the brilliance of all that he is, the woman departed. And so she made her transition and stepped forward in the heavens to shepherd this man's journey.

How wonderful that their time together in life had brought them to resonate harmonically with one another, enabling her to blend with him effortlessly from beyond! How wonderful that her own divine consciousness expanded to its pure angelic state upon her transition and that this breadth of wisdom, guidance and inspiration became an intimate part of her connection with him! How very wonderful!

*Soaring with Angels*

And so today our dear man continues his spectacular expansion. Though his life continues to appear common, it is nothing short of extraordinary. For today he walks as a man and soars with the angels. With each breath, he inhales a greater surety of his divinity. His wisdom inspires minds. His compassion opens hearts. His peace alters space. He is magnificent in his unfolding, the unfurling of his angel wings.

# *My Dream*

When I was about seven years old, I had a dream. It was so clear that the next morning I described it to my mother. Every detail. Every feeling.

I was an older man. I felt my age—not in the way that an old man may feel weary, but in the way that a child would experience himself in a moment to be an older man. I felt expanded and wise. I felt strong and sure. I felt kind and gentle.

I was walking in the woods at night. There were tall trees with long thin trunks and others with large knotty trunks. There must have been a lit moon, because I could see things quite clearly around me.

Three younger men were walking with me. Just behind me. I knew them. There was silence between us, the frosted leaves crisp beneath our steps.

I remember the fragrance of the woods—a wonderful sweet smell that I loved. I felt the life about me, particularly in the air. I breathed it knowingly. I felt very much at peace. Safe and comfortable.

As I walked forward toward one beautiful tree, its coarse bark just within reach, I turned. In the same moment of my turning one of the men thrust a blade into my stomach. He thrust again into my heart. Next into my neck. And into my head. This was how I experienced it. It happened very quickly. Suddenly.

There was no pain, only a knowing. My awareness followed the thrusts from my abdomen to my heart to my throat to my skull. I felt myself become light and I immediately spun as if in a tornado. Up through the top of my head and on into the sky. Spinning faster and faster in a brilliant kaleidoscope of colors until I exploded into awesome light.

This is etched in my memory. It is etched in my experience. The experience of becoming this most powerful vortex as I spiraled rapidly skyward. And then the final moment of bursting into a great, white, blinding light.

I knew I had experienced my death. Though I described it to my mother as *that man's death*, I knew it was mine. I am grateful that she asked me to write it down. I am grateful that she honored the experience enough to cherish it and help me anchor it in my being.

I understand now that this memory served to remind me of the place to which we return at the end of our human lives. My consciousness in that lifetime was expanded. So there was a fluid return to the divine realm upon my passing.

I have pondered the effect of this dream upon my being. Not only did it ground within me a knowing of our true home and the inner knowing that nothing would ever prevent me from returning to that divine realm, but because of this knowing, I have become one who is not fearful of seeking and exploring outside the field of what is *safe* and *acceptable*. I have never been threatened by notions of hell or sin or sacrilege. And so I have been free. Deep within my being, free.

This beautiful dream was a gift. And it was seeded in my memory in childhood so that I could be open to the possibility of self discovery available to me in this life.

It was only a matter of patiently awaiting the brilliantly orchestrated unfolding of my life that would reveal to me the occasions for choosing to expand into divinity.

# *Yasmin*

Once I was young and carefree and living in Seattle. I was in college finishing off a degree that hadn't gone so well the first time around in Montreal. Seattle was looking better. I was happy with good friends, living in a good place.

I was exploring my freedom. Exploring myself. I had a decent job and was doing well in school, studying philosophy and economics and religion.

Prior to this, I had been trapped under the weight of disappointment. I had been caught beneath the weight of my own insecurities and adopted judgments. I had been trapped for quite some time beneath a resistance to do what was expected of me. Knowing it would be a dead end road. Knowing it would only bring me more apathy.

And I had been hypnotized to numbness, feeling like a child, incapable of picking myself up and moving forward in life.

I now see that I was trapped beneath a blanket that was woven by others and yet had somehow become my refuge, my safety and my identity. Isn't this what a security blanket is? Something that you are given as a child to keep you safe, but to which you might become strangely and unwittingly attached?

This is what happens to most of humanity when we adopt ideas and beliefs in childhood and proceed to unconsciously define our reality and ourselves by these notions throughout our adult lives.

So we put on our suits and go out into the world, all the while cradling our fuzzy, worn, stained security blankets in the crook of our necks. Feeling lost without them.

In truth it is only our limited perceptions that lead us to believe it is our environment and our rearing that entrap us. The reality is that our lives are magically orchestrated to reflect to us that which we choose to experience as part of our grand adventure of life. As part of our grand adventure of self discovery.

It was Christmas-time when I heard some sad news. A friend had been in a terrible car accident. Yasmin had not survived. I remember my shock. Such a young and beautiful girl. Suddenly gone. What must the family be going through?

I immediately returned home. There were still many people gathering at her family's house that evening. When I arrived there was so much grief, it was like hitting a wall of despair. Yasmin's mother had always been a most kind and sensitive woman, one who wore her heart on her sleeve. She had been struck badly by her loss. I still remember encountering Yasmin's sister. She pulled me close and sobbed.

I do not wish to diminish the loss this dear family experienced by jumping into my story right away. So let me tell you that this event impacted them deeply for many years. They are a beautiful family and life has continued for each of them. And they forever hold a special place in their hearts for their dear daughter and sister. Yasmin is remembered for the joyful, bubbly, mischievous girl that she was. She will ever be kept in mind and heart as fun-loving, filling the lives of her family and friends with laughter and hope as she embraced the wonderful exploration of her young life. She was adventurous and free and she left many cherished memories.

For me, this event had a curiously profound impact that would echo for years. It was a pivotal moment in my life. Though I too was saddened by Yasmin's death, I was most profoundly struck with confusion. Death had never before impacted me so significantly.

With all those around me who were affected by the tragedy, questions abounded. These were spiritual and philosophical questions. Mostly they arose from within my own heart.

What was the reason God had taken her? Had she done something wrong? Why was her family being made to suffer? For someone so young and full of life, why should her life be cut short? If God was indeed just, where was the justice? And why couldn't I see it?

I took it upon myself to ask the hard questions of our community's religious scholars. I was relentless. But with every question I asked and every response I received, I grew more restless. More dissatisfied.

What absolutely maddened me was that each scholar offered different responses to the same questions. Not mildly different, but dramatically different. As if there was no clear cut answer to any question of faith or of death, of God or of justice. As if everything could be interpreted by whoever was doing the interpreting.

Because I had been brought up with such a strong religious foundation, I was never afraid to challenge the scholars. I wasn't afraid to debate with them and offer my thoughts based upon my understanding of our faith.

But in this case and because I was so persistent, ultimately I was told that some things are not meant to be understood. That some things are in the hands of God and are not within our ability to comprehend. That to question these things was to lack faith.

For the first time in my life, I categorically rejected what I was being told. I knew without any doubt whatsoever that there *were* answers to my questions. This was a knowing that arose within me and could not be denied.

I had just come to the shocking realization that those few who had been charged with being the interpreters of our faith had no answers of substance to offer. On this subject, they were simply spouting platitudes and speaking from intellectual exegeses without truly *knowing* what they spoke of.

And I pondered, if they could not respond to these most basic, most elementary, yet most important issues of faith, then what good was their knowledge?

An overwhelming impulse took me over at that moment. All of a sudden, my mind was predominantly preoccupied with issues of religion, issues of belief, issues of life. Questions of God, the human identity, the soul. The nature of death. Of the afterlife. Of the possibility of reincarnation. Of divine justice. And on and on.

I took every opportunity to seek out answers at school, in the library, with my professors. But this kept leading to greater and greater confusion. Religious texts revealed teachings that were prosaic, regurgitated and construed. I discovered how much I already understood and realized that what I was seeking was beyond the ken of these thinkers.

I felt disappointed and disillusioned. I acknowledged a rising contempt for those who pretended to know, those whose sources of knowledge were simply academic and not substantive or experiential.

At the same time, I was enlivened by hunger. I had become so overwhelmed by my search for truth that I was overcome by a one-minded passion for only this. I became the fool who set aside everything in his quest for the pot of gold. And so I was desperately chasing rainbows.

Throughout this time in my life, my unwavering faith in all I had known was replaced with an unwavering belief that the answers were out there. I never lost sight of this, never lost hope that I could come to know the deeper truths that would make sense out of the many questions I had.

And I never lost my love of God.

I know today that this sense of entitlement that I felt—that I had a *right* to know the truth—was my saving grace. It defined me. It clarified that I was *worthy* of knowing the truth. And in that moment, it made me worthy.

As I look back upon myself in those days of searching, I recognize that I was impulsed with the seeds of the wisdom to manifest my desires without even understanding the effect of my intentions. *Ask, and ye shall receive.*

Let me explain. My unflinching resolve to seek clarity and break free of confusion and limited beliefs brought me exactly that—the opportunity to experience clarity and to become one with truth. And so doors began to open that would reveal to me that which I was seeking. Doors which until then had merely been clouds in the sky.

# The Great White Book

As a child, my mother had maintained a collection of books by Ruth Montgomery, the great American psychic who wrote about the afterlife. In the months following Yasmin's death as I became more and more pre-occupied with my *unanswered* questions, I was reminded of these books. And I devoured them anew.

However, as wonderful as it was to discover the answers to so many of my questions about life after death, I was only further stimulated to seek out the meaning behind the deeper matters that were haunting me.

One afternoon, I was browsing my favorite used bookstore when—all of a sudden—a book fell off a shelf and knocked me in the head. It was a white book, simply titled *Ramtha*. Little did I know at the time that this book would open my eyes to unconsidered ideas and amazing truths. Little did I know that I was venturing into a realm so magical and unbelievable that it would rattle all my perceptions and dazzle me with fantastical possibilities. Little did I know that the very fantasies that I used to scoff at as juvenile and imaginary would become my greatest realities.

I read the book from cover to cover in my first sitting. I was stupefied by the words. Ramtha claimed to be a discarnate soul who in his last lifetime had been the great lord Ram from the Hindu belief system. He spoke by way of temporarily inhabiting the body of a beautiful blonde woman named JZ Knight. He told an amazing tale of his life and times that was very engaging and inspiring to read.

I wasn't sure if I believed it. It didn't track as historically correct. But it didn't matter. What was important was that he spoke of topics that touched my heart. The very subjects that I had been yearning and hungering to understand. He spoke of them with clarity and surety. He spoke of them in a manner that broke through the mysteries and made them seem obvious. I was inspired and my heart was lightened. I knew I had found truth.

I soon discovered that JZ lived in a small town less than two hours from me. From her property, she conducted retreats for the many people who chose to experience Ramtha and benefit from his wisdom.

I registered for a two-day workshop some weeks away. I was so anxious, so eager, so very excited. I remember being fascinated by virtually everything I experienced. There were one thousand people in attendance—including several celebrities I recognized.

At first sight I would have described the site as rough and most of the attendees and staff as bumpkins. I felt very much out of my element. I laugh as I reflect upon myself back then. My limited life experiences had resulted in a very immature appreciation of people and the world.

Despite the discomfort, I was thrilled to be there. I was among a horde of people who had been led into a large barn where each of us staked out a three-foot by six-foot spot on the dirt floor.

Our materials list had included all the necessary items. So I followed those around me and lay down my blanket and my sleeping bag, a pillow, my notebook and pens, and a water bottle. It was cold so I kept my sweater on. Some were wearing sweat pants. I felt foolish in mine.

It was quite some time before people settled down and the barn filled. Everyone was seated on their cushions—me on my pillow—and more-or-less facing a raised platform upon which sat a beautiful and elegant armchair and a low table carrying flowers, a pitcher of water and a glass. I was quite close to all of this.

The stage was set. I was excited, and I remember thinking that I really didn't know what to expect.

Someone announced that Ramtha was on his way. My mind was spinning. How did this work? Ramtha was a centuries-old being. How would he come? Was JZ coming? How would he enter into her body?

All of a sudden people were standing. Applause gushed. At the far end of the barn, a blonde woman wearing a white and gold robe was marching down the aisle.

That was JZ!

But as I looked at her beautiful face, it was not the face of a woman. The features were transformed—her face appeared ruddy and full and masculine. As was her gait.

There was an intensity about her. And then as she approached the stage, her eyes met mine and held for a beat. In that moment I felt an overwhelming rush sweep up through my body. My heart was beating hard and had become full. I felt an incredible sense of awe and wonder. This was Ramtha. I felt his power and his magnificence—he radiated brilliance and it was palpable. I was dumbfounded.

The weekend was more than I could have dreamed it would be. Ramtha lectured for hours on topics dear to my heart. Everything that I had been searching for—here were the answers.

The most important thing was that what he said resonated as truth to me. It was amazing to be in his presence. He was vibrant and bold. At times his speech bordered on harsh and absolute. And there was no ambiguity.

Ramtha explained over and over again that the most fundamental principle of his teaching was that we are all divine. We are Gods. We are all Gods! He taught us a form of meditation that he referred to as *the breath*. It was a powerful tool that would accelerate our process of enlightenment. I remember thinking, *how remarkable that I am in the presence of an enlightened being who is willing to show me how to achieve that same lofty state!* He played games with us. Games that were designed to prove to us that we were capable of experiencing the truth of ourselves *for ourselves*.

He spoke of the cause of all of our common and personal ills, of the real purpose of life, of the true nature of God. He spoke about time and space and their true relevance in the grand nature of life. Topic after topic was profound and stimulating. I was riveted and impassioned. Keen to experience the things of which he spoke.

# Lost In the Dark

I spent another year with Ramtha's teachings before moving on. My journey led me to New York, then the Carolinas. I ended up settling in a small town nestled against the Smoky Mountains. There, I met many like minded seekers. I also met Denise, a beautiful blonde belle from Texas who I fell quickly in love with.

She was staying with her parents following her arrival in town. Kay and Jim were very loving people. They doted on Denise, and they treated me as if I was one of their own. It was a magical time for me, and I have many fond memories of my days there.

One evening after dinner we were all seated in the living room when Kay suddenly noticed something odd. Denise had been sitting on the floor and had apparently disengaged from our conversation. All of a sudden she started swaying back and forth. She was clearly in an altered state and visibly uncomfortable. Kay reached over to her and tried to get her attention.

But Denise was not quite present.

"There is someone with us," Kay said. These women were very psychic—and extremely open. "She wants to talk to us." *What?! What on earth?!* I thought. Kay gave quick instructions. "Jim, I'll let her come through me. Denise isn't strong enough—hold onto her until she's okay."

The next moment Kay was moving into a deep, deep state. Her breaths getting more and more shallow. At the same time, Denise came out of her trance. Jim explained to her what was happening then moved back to the sofa to support Kay, whose body was now slumping over.

It was clear that a spirit had taken over Kay's body. She was whimpering. Sobbing weakly and as if completely devoid of energy and very frightened—like a little child lost in the dark.

In that moment a calm overtook me. A calm and a knowing. I started speaking without thinking. I mean that. This was perhaps my first experience of consciously following an unconscious impulse. Of bypassing the monkey mind and trusting my intuition. And yet I was very present in that moment and in that experience. It felt different and I felt different. And it all happened in a moment.

"Yasmin? Is that you?" The words just tumbled out of my mouth. How did I even know it was her?

"Yes," she said. She was still whimpering.

"Why are you here?" I remember asking.

"You are the only one who will talk to me," she answered. Her voice was weak and full of hesitation and grief. "Everyone ignores me. I'm cold. I'm so cold. I'm sorry. I'm so sorry."

In a flash, I realized that she was in limbo—that she hadn't acknowledged her death. "Yasmin, tell me the last thing you remember."

She said nothing but sobbed.

"Yasmin, you were driving your car home from work. Do you remember?"

"Yes," she said.

I spoke next in a very delicate and gentle voice. "You were in a horrible car crash. Do you remember?"

She said nothing. But her whimpering had stopped. She was listening.

"Yasmin, your body was injured so badly that it wasn't able to hold you anymore." I had spoken the words gently yet deliberately. There was a long silence. "Did you see the light?" I persisted.

"No," she answered finally. I felt her fear was returning.

"Ask to see the light now, Yasmin. Ask."

"I can't see anything. It's so dark. I'm so cold." Her anxiety increased and she began whimpering again. She was so terrified.

"Yasmin, do you remember my grandfather?" The words spilled from my mouth. God knows from where. It was brilliant and inspired and perfect. My grandfather had passed on some fifteen years earlier. "Ask him to show himself to you. Please, Yasmin, ask him to show himself to you."

The next words out of her mouth stunned me. "He looks so young." The stress in her voice was gone. In its place was wonderment. There was more silence.

"Go with him Yasmin. You're safe now. He will explain everything to you. Go with him." She was already engaged with him while I spoke these final words. I realized this.

I was stunned. We were all stunned. There was not a lot of talk that night. Kay was completely exhausted and Jim carried her up to their bedroom. Denise and I sat together for a few minutes, but my thoughts were awhirl. And my emotions—they were raw. Only shock kept me from crying. It occurs to me now as I recall the experience that my heart had lightened. For some two and a half years I had been carrying sadness in my heart. It strikes me that much of this grief was actually Yasmin's. I had attached myself to her soon after her death. And I was in part the vehicle for her expression. It was all so amazing. At the time I was numb. There was so much here for me to grasp and comprehend.

I bless Kay and Denise and Jim. I love them, I honor them, I thank them. That evening they performed an act of pure compassion. Of pure love and mercy. They freed a soul on that night, a dear and sweet young girl who lost herself in the moment of her transition. They brought her to the light. They will forever have a special place in my heart for what they did for me that night and on many other days and nights. They are my family.

Several days after my encounter with Yasmin's spirit, I traveled to Clarkesville to visit my dear Elmarilla. Yasmin was very much on my mind.

What an incredible experience it had been! Elmarilla lovingly answered my many questions. She explained that Yasmin had been driving down a steep hill and had been distracted when she was changing the radio station—or doing some such thing. Her car had veered into the opposing lane and struck a van driving in the opposite direction. It was a violent crash and Yasmin was killed instantly.

I asked why she hadn't realized her own death. Elmarilla told me that Yasmin did experience herself looking down at her dead body. But this confused her. And because she did not have an understanding of what happens to someone upon death, she dismissed the sight and remained attached to her life.

She had attempted to be with her family and communicate with them. But she felt that they were ignoring her. She began to blame herself and concocted a host of reasons why her family and closest friends were upset with her. I was concerned that she had experienced that terrifying trauma for two and a half years. But time had not impacted her. The entire experience had lasted but one moment for her.

I was reminded that it was just an accident. For years I had been struggling to understand why. *Why was her beautiful life cut so short?* And Elmarilla's simple answer was, "It was just a careless mistake." Ah! So there was no punishment being meted out. No grand scheme at play. This was just a life being lived. I am quite sure there is more to her personal story that may decipher the puzzle of her experience, of her life and of her death. But that's for her. It is her personal story. For me, this was all I needed to know.

It had been a few days since Yasmin crossed over. And Elmarilla told me that she had regained her strength. That she was a vibrant and eager spirit. She was busying herself with her life review and would soon be ready to prepare for another life experience. She was eager to do so. This was her passion and her desire. And she would return soon.

## *Urimi*

*Urimi descended from the heavens in a gentle spiral.*
*She had been soaring on high for ages,*
*Her wings spread wide, tip-feathers reaching outward*
*Extending her span.*
*Breaking through the clouds, a beautiful island beckoned*
*earnestly amidst a sea of others.*
*This isle sparkled brilliantly in the bluest of waters.*

*As she landed atop the tallest palm,*
*Its dates plump and sweet,*
*The island shuddered.*
*Urimi brought with her*
*The magnificence of her heavenly breadth.*
*And as she plucked a ripened date,*
*Urimi herself shuddered.*
*The delight and wonder of the island's bounty*
*Enthralled her.*

*What an extraordinary thing those two do share!*
*Breadth and bounty,*
*Heaven and earth.*

*Lucky Urimi.*
*Lucky Island*

# The Crystalline Pyramid

Elmarilla introduced a wonderful metaphor to help me understand who we truly are. When I first met her, I was a wide-eyed seeker who was questioning everything I knew to be true. I had been brought up with a very clear set of beliefs. My family, my religion and my environment had consistently reinforced my ideas about life, God and humankind.

But a sudden event in my life and a powerful compulsion deep within led me onto a magical journey of discovery.

I began to question everything that I had been brought up to believe. Everything that I did believe.

And one afternoon while enjoying a bowl of Elmarilla's wonderful cheddar corn chowder, she explained to me the truth of who we are.

*Imagine yourself as a beautiful, massive, crystalline pyramid. The many different aspects that make up the totality of your being are contained within this design. You are much, much more than you think yourself to be.*

*Consider that your present experience as Shams-Tabriz is one block within your pyramid. In this moment you still experience yourself as distinct, as unique, as individual. In fact you are not.*

*You are all of the different blocks within your pyramid. You have a breadth of experience that encompasses all that is within the realm of experience. You are both saint and sinner. Peasant and prince. Tyrant and victim.*

*While you experience yourself in time and space, in truth the pyramid contains all that you are in the Now.*

*Also within your pyramid are realms of consciousness that are angelic, that originate from other places, that would be deemed to be of a much more enlightened state than humankind.*

*Now at the very top of your pyramid is your capstone. This is the part of you that knows the totality and wholeness of your pyramid. That is intimately connected with the source of all that is. That is equally connected with the capstone of all pyramids. We can call this the King and Queen of your pyramid.*

*It recognizes the wholeness of all the blocks and acts as the master of your kingdom. It loves without judgment. Without condition. It knows all experience. It embraces all experience. And it rules your kingdom with wisdom and justice.*

*Since it recognizes the multiplicity of experiences as part of its magnificent totality, it does not condemn. It loves. And just as it experiences this beneficence and mercy for its own kingdom, it naturally experiences this same compassion and kindness for the kingdoms of all others.*

I remember my fascination with these images. Elmarilla had gifted me a great insight. I asked her many questions and interrupted her often. But she treated me as her son, patiently and wisely explaining until I understood.

I still remember the warmth of that afternoon. Sitting inside her home with the most vivid colors about us. The fall leaves outside. The prismic brilliance inside—her home was full of crystals that played with light. As I reflect upon it now, the setting was impeccable. It was as if we were seated within an actual crystalline pyramid. How funny that I didn't realize it until this moment!

I have repeated Elmarilla's words often to myself and to others over the years. It is a great wisdom that offers us an insight into the reality of that which we are. It has been many years since I first found friendship with Elmarilla.

Only of late have I truly acknowledged that as Shams-Tabriz I am consciously dwelling in my pyramid. Only now have I embraced the understanding that I will reside ever more consciously in my capstone.

It has not been like flipping a switch from off to on. It has been like the breaking of dawn with clouds and trees to the east. In one moment the sun has arrived, visible and brilliant in its fresh radiance. In the next a low-lying cloud has hidden the light. Then again the sun emerges, casting only warmth. The next, a tree obscures the vista. So I run out from behind the branches in my wish to bask in the sun.

And so it has been for me.

But the course has been set. My choice is firm and resolute. And my sun continues to break free of its occlusions, revealing to me a greater and greater experience of my wholeness. I look upon myself with compassion and patience in this moment and can envision me wearing my robe, donning my crown, sitting upon my throne—the King and Queen of my pyramid.

# We Are the Same

Despite being raised in a very worldly and open-minded-family, there was much for me to learn about my distorted perceptions. Life had been defined as a struggle. This was something I had heard often from a young age. And so the focus became that—struggle.

Life was hard, and I wondered if I was doing something wrong if I experienced life to be easy. For things to come easily and effortlessly, without trial and without struggle… well, this simply was not noble. Was it?

It took a while before I seriously and honestly began examining my beliefs. And when I started doing this, my whole world came apart.

I went from depending on religious and parental lore as my guiding principles to seeking far and wide for wisdom to provide me with guidance, wisdom that I came to discover was clearly both more personal as well as more relevant and inspired.

All of a sudden, I realized I was important as an individual. Not only were my grand questions about life and the hereafter met with meaningful insight, not only was I overwhelmed by miraculous contact with angels and departed family members, but the seeming minutiae of my life were welcome topics of conversation with these same inspired beings.

A shift began within me. I came to see myself differently. As a significant member of humanity for whom the angels and spirit masters would offer guidance and insight. As someone whose hopes and dreams were precious.

I received an important glimpse into the possibilities for mankind. Specifically, I had been granted a glimpse at what lay ahead for me in my life. The possibility to rise to the awareness of the saints who have stepped beyond the limited perspectives of their time and into the greater awareness that embraces us all.

It was this initial awakening that has lit my path all these days since. This deep knowing that I am—and that we all are—blessed and divine beings having a human experience. Beings with the divine gift of being creators. It became my reality evermore clearly that despite whether or not we are aware of this truth, we are creators in every moment of our experience. Even the suffering we experience in our lives is our creation.

And rest assured, I have asked before, "How is it that I have created this suffering? It cannot be true! I would not create suffering for myself! It makes no sense! I seek love, I seek joy, I seek abundance and prosperity. So how can you tell me that I create my suffering?"

But I am here to tell you that I now understand. I understand fully how all of my experiences of old, all the distress and misery, sadness and frustration, anger and disgust, each of these was brought about by my ignorance, by my resistance, and by my fears.

And it is true. What I did not know—all of my misperceptions about myself and life—caused me to create for myself a life of chaos and dis-ease.

And the only saving grace is that there were a choice few events in my life—remarkable and notable events, to be sure—that compelled me from deep within the core of my being to seek to understand more.

Today as I reflect upon this, I envision it as if an angel stepped deep into the recesses of my cloistered darkness and gently tapped me on the shoulder as he opened his eyes to show me the soft brilliance of his divine light. And in that moment, he whispered to me,

*You are the same, my brother. We are all the same.*

Does this make sense to you? Is reading this book one of your choice events? Does what you read in this moment prompt you to know more, to be more? Can you acknowledge that you do not know all that there is to know about life and who you are? And can you admit to yourself that you deserve to know?

Can you step beyond the limiting definitions that we have placed upon humankind and conceive of yourself as truly a seed of the divine? And can you summon the courage and the willingness to explore this possibility? Can you set aside your fears of punishment and retribution from the many communities that society has collected and truly embrace your own hunger for knowledge and understanding?

I have done this. And believe me when I tell you that I have faced harsh judgments from those I have loved and admired. But I have persisted because my heart told me there is more than the insignificant life of suffering and punishment. There is more to life than being a sheep in a flock—even a black sheep. There is more to life than being duty bound and obligated and devoid of true understanding.

I have trusted my heart when it has revealed these impulses to me. And though the many forces around us may flow downstream, I have held my gaze upon the distant mountaintop and I have pressed against the currents and fought to swim towards the pinnacle of truth.

It has been a lonely journey at times, a seemingly impossible journey at times, an agonizing journey at times. But it has continued to be my journey at all times.

There is something I have never lacked—the courage to stand apart, if necessary, to discover the truth. I have been blessed with a deep and abiding awareness that there is truly no wrong that I can do in life, nothing that will be punishable by condemnation in the flames of hell or any such thing. And this knowing I attribute in part to a dream—the reminder that my home resides far up in the heavens in a place of spectacular light and overflowing love.

> *I have lived in a coop,*
> *Dined on only chicken feed for many moons,*
> *And now?*
> *How nice this bit of caviar.*

# Still the Mind

The world needs to learn how to meditate. I don't mean to paint a picture of a red and white frock-clad society of ascetics roaming the streets, moaning mantras and grinning lamely while sipping Coca-Cola on a street corner. This certainly would be amusing to witness, but it is not what is needed. What I refer to is the community of man experiencing life fully—but with clear minds. Mindfully paying attention.

I was gifted the experience of spending over a year engaged with a group of monks. They were a sweet bunch. One beautiful girl captured my heart with her sweetness and grace. She became my inspiration and often my devotion. I will forever cherish her brilliance.

The monks were my friends and they were my teachers. They taught me the beautiful art of stilling the mind. In truth, this is not something we need to learn. For this is our natural, divine state of being at its very core. Thought is the first manifestation from this core. And from thought springs all things seen and unseen, material and spiritual, everything that emerges from the original pure and powerful creative thought of God.

It is through our many, many lifetimes of human experience… Let me pause here for a moment. It would be wise for you to begin to understand that as brilliant as the human experience is, it's not the only show in town. There are an endless number of other worlds, dimensions, and realities open for us to experience. But for the purpose of our discussion, I will refer to our human experience.

As I was saying, it is through our many, many lifetimes of human experience that we have built up endless fodder for our monkey minds. Memories and judgments and fears. Resistance and mistrust and confusion. Frustration and resentment and loss. Even the joys and the loves and the laughter of our lives. These all exist as emotional memories within our being.

The teaching of the monks was to come to watch your thoughts, to disengage from the thoughts.

It's a mind-boggling moment when you begin to pay attention to the intense and sometimes frenetic workings of the monkey mind. It was at the same time amazing and amusing to begin the practice these monks taught. The idea was not to attach yourself to any one thought but simply to watch them.

At first, it felt as though within a moment of practice my monkey mind would glom onto a thought, be it a memory or an emotion—something as simple as feeling hunger or questioning if I was watching properly—and before I knew it dozens of minutes would have passed before I realized that a train of thoughts had taken me from watching thoughts to surfing them. And the moment I would catch myself, the instruction was to return immediately to watching.

This was a very significant aspect of my learning.

The monkey mind prevents you from experiencing fully what is in the moment! Some of you may not even understand this.

Most of humanity is so clouded by fears, preconditioned notions and past experiences that define reactions that it would be fair to state that on a scale of zombie to angel we're operating mostly as zombies. While angels are ones who dwell in the full knowing and the full experience of their divine nature.

We on the other end of the scale are muted to the true reality that surrounds us. We are muted to the depth of experience that is life. We are muted to the fullness and the splendor that defines us. We are muted. We are zombies.

As I practiced paying attention, I began to detach myself from the numbing effects of the constant thoughts that distracted me from smelling the roses. And a magical thing began to happen. *I began to smell roses.* I began to discover a depth to life that I hadn't noticed before.

The monks taught detachment from *all* thoughts. I came to a point in my practice where I became the watcher watching myself watching my thoughts. Funny that.

Today, I am far too fascinated by the possibilities that the creation of this human realm promises—man walking as god, god walking as man in a brilliant experience of creativity and discovery, forever expanding the divine kingdom.

The gifts I speak of when I refer to stilling the mind, when I refer to learning how to meditate, are the gifts that emerge when you are clear enough in your thoughts to truly pay attention to what is going on in your life.

For if you pay attention to your thoughts, if you do not simply detach yourself and ignore them, you will reveal to yourself the thoughts, and perhaps more importantly the feelings and emotions, that you are experiencing. And these are the gems. For these reveal to you what fears you may have, what resistances, what anxieties, what angers, what judgments.

If you practice this with honesty and truthfulness, with what I like to refer to as *complete transparency*, you reveal the truth of yourself to yourself. You will discover who you are in this moment of revealing.

It is not for you to judge yourself. It is not for you to say, "Ah, I'm a horrible person because I notice that I do not experience love in every moment." It is simply for you to notice what it is in truth that you do feel. And then allow yourself to go deeper. There could be any number of reasons why you are feeling what you're feeling.

It could be that your experience brings up frustration. Why would you suppress the emotion?

Because you deem yourself to be not precious? Because you deem yourself to be unworthy? Because you judge anger? You deem it to be an unholy emotion?

*Do not judge yourself!* Face the resistance that you have to examine yourself, and begin to look more closely at your behaviors. And ask yourself why? What compels you? Sometimes you may find a seed of understanding in your life—in a childhood experience, in the way you were raised, in your relationships. Sometimes you will not. Okay. But again, do not judge.

Remember always that you are the master creator of your life and your experiences. You have orchestrated this all for your greater learning.

If you will remember that your core intention is to discover your divinity and to surrender and forgive all that is within you that defies this knowing, then it will be easier. For you will know that this is the greater path. You will know that nothing has more power over you than your desire to know yourself fully and then to *be* that knowing.

Some of you will encounter obstacles within your being that have been built up for many, many lifetimes. It is true. You recreate lifetime after lifetime—different stories and different characters, but the same core experience—simply to continue to give yourself the opportunity to see yourself and others through divine eyes.

And know one thing. In this lifetime if you do not pay attention to your feelings and ignore what they aim to reveal to you, then you will continue to create lifetimes for yourself for the very same purpose. To overcome limitation.

For you are divine. And divinity is unlimited.

As you allow your feelings to surface you will find that some of them have stories to which they can be easily linked, while others do not. Perhaps the stories are from another time, another life. Perhaps the stories are all too similar and so the details lose their relevance.

Some of the stories it serves you well to discover, to remember, to reveal to yourself. For in them is a pearl of truth, a wisdom and a learning that can propel you to a higher level of awareness, to a greater knowing of yourself. Some of them you may only come to know in fragments, for this is all that is required to reveal what is to be known. What is to be forgiven. What is to be integrated.

And some of the stories you may not come to know at all in this lifetime. So be it. Trust that your own unique divine guidance guides this too— and guides it wisely and to the greatest of benefits.

But I do beseech you, pay attention to what you feel as you go about your life. Pay attention, for life will reveal to you all that needs revealing for you to step ever more boldly, ever more confidently onto your path to divinity.

Set this as your principal goal—to fully know yourself, to fully be the divine blessed being that you are, and to come to see that same blessed reality in all of humanity. Others may not see it of themselves, but this will not prevent you from knowing it of them and seeing it within them.

And set also as your wish that all will be revealed with the guidance and the love, the strength and the support, of the highest, finest realms of consciousness—what I refer to as the realm of the Angels. For this will protect you and secure you.

This intention will ensure your path is lined with gold. And though it may be rocky and steep, slippery and seemingly impossible, it will be lighted from above. And you will know that the grace of God cloaks you on your journey.

# *Pay Attention!*

My experience with the monks was wonderful. In a very short time, the practice taught me to still the mind. Today, I reside in my heart. My mind serves my heart—but it is not my mind through which I experience life. My heart is my present-moment reality. My heart is my experience in the now. It is evermore clean and clear and unburdened by past impressions, unconscious behaviors and old responses. As I have done this, my feelings of self and my observations of others have revealed a great many things to me.

Once, someone I knew was behaving harshly, with hostility and contempt. By observing her condition *without judgment,* I became aware that the stress she was experiencing was a symptom of the effort she exerted to avoid looking within. I will elucidate.

She had found herself in a very unhappy situation. And certain events had unfolded in her life to bring this to the forefront of her present-moment experience without a host of other distractions to serve as a buffer. And so her feelings were raw and unavoidable.

In the past, it had been easy to project these feelings onto others in her life, to blame them for having been the cause of her condition. And this had been enough to provide her a temporary sense of relief. In truth, it merely provided her a sense of justification and self-righteousness which gave her only a false sense of relief.

This has been mankind's pattern for ages. We comfort our false ego by assigning our own manifestations of guilt onto others. And so others become the guilty, the blameworthy, the faulty.

But due to the concentrated focus on her sad condition that life had orchestrated for her, it was not enough to blame others and find solace in the belief that others were responsible for ruining her life. And so the emotions continued to well up. In time it had become so overpowering for her that she became a rather difficult person to be around. Her hostile judgments even extended to matters completely unrelated to her own issues. It was a if she needed to keep firing shots wildly simply to deafen herself from the voice within.

You will see this same pattern in yourself and those around you. You go about your lives avoiding your shadows, fearful of what they may reveal to you. And so it becomes easier to project your secret judgments onto others rather than acknowledge the truth of their origin and look within.

And yet if you were to pay attention to what is truly going on, you would realize that your actions and behaviors are serving only one master—the false ego. The part of you that desperately wants to avoid looking within yourself for the cause of your perceived failings. The part of you that is fearful of looking within, dreading all the monsters lurking in the shadows, horrified by the prospect that all the pain and suffering of lifetimes might have been your own creation.

Understand that the false ego is not a part of you that is to be judged. There is no value whatsoever in judgment. None. The false ego is simply a term I use to denote the conscious expression of yourself that is not aware of your divinity, that adopts a host of construed behaviors and beliefs to create a shroud of falseness that reinforces your sense of separation, unworthiness and ungodliness.

The false ego is not meant to be surgically removed from you—it is not a cancer within your being. Your false ego is simply out of balance and in the dark. The objective is to heal the false ego through compassion and understanding, truthfulness and forgiveness, surrender and trust. And as this happens, the ego evermore comes into harmony with the truth of who you are and you will emerge to express wholly with what I like to refer to as a *healthy ego*.

In the season of our evolution that is now, we are in the midst of ever-expanding energies enriching our world. This planet is shifting. It is undergoing its own enlightenment. It is raising its harmonic, vibrational frequencies to accommodate ever higher consciousnesses in its inhabitants.

Humankind consists of electromagnetic beings. Earth is an electromagnetic organism. Every element of creation is this and is designed to resonate at its own frequency. As the planet has undergone evolution, it has gradually raised its frequency in concert with the evolution of humanity. In our present time, we are witness to a rapid expansion of energies upon this plane. This not only prompts an equally rapid evolution of the world in which we live but also of all of life within this realm. And vice versa. The timely evolution of the human experience is extending out of the grounded reality of each consciously enlightened person and affecting others as well as the world itself.

This rapid influx of higher, finer frequencies transforming our world impacts each one of us profoundly. Those of us who have attended to our spiritual inclinations and have open heartedly and open mindedly sought to understand the truth of our divine nature have prepared ourselves for the time that is now. We are equally impacted by the global and personal energetic shifts but have learned how to expand with them, in consciousness and in body.

However the majority of humankind that has maintained distance from such possibilities and such realities are today beginning to find themselves facing seemingly insurmountable odds. They are being brought to question their choices, their actions, their relationships, their beliefs and their faith. They are finding themselves grasping to make sense of all the confusion in their lives. Their active minds are struggling to contain the myriad of emotions, thoughts and other subtle experiences they are surely facing.

Picture the medical treatment for kidney stones. Pulses of high frequency sound waves are directed at the stones intending to shatter them into tiny fragments that can be easily released by the kidneys—shock wave therapy.

Now imagine that your lifetimes of judgments and sorrows, pains and fears, false notions and faithlessness reside within you as dense clumps of darkness in both your energetic body and your physical being. Imagine that from beyond our realm, from the place of our angelic heritage and the places of wisdom and guidance throughout creation, there emerges shock waves directed at cleansing humanity and the planet of all of its dis-ease.

But you are not a kidney. Your attachment to your judgments, fears, notions, beliefs and behaviors are most strong. You relate to them, and they form your identity. And without another identity to which you may seek to attach yourself, your greatest defenses will emerge to protect your false ego.

So now picture a great battle waging between the forces of divine brilliance that are compelling your evolution and the forces of individual and collective resistance within mankind that are fearful of the change that is upon us. The result of this battle is chaos. The only resolution is to trust the forces of brilliance and surrender to their transformative powers. Short of this, chaos will prevail. And such is the state of much of mankind today.

By being courageous enough to make choices to expand your experience of self, you will redefine yourself, deciding who you are and what you are in every moment. Begin by choosing things within your environment that are within your perceived control. Choose where to go. Choose who to spend time with. Choose what to do. Choose what makes you happy. For that is integral.

Begin to discover what makes you happy.

Many of you are so distant from the truth of what inspires you, what motivates you, what pleases you, what brings you joy, what fulfills you, what expands you. Most are far away from even being able to grasp these notions.

You are so conditioned with a whole host of different belief systems and ideologies and patterns of behavior, that you don't even know how to begin making these choices. And yet it's critical that you do. It is the miracle of choice.

In contemplating your choices, seek to honor yourself. Seek to recognize who you are. Seek to experience the expanded possibility of yourself.

Surrender yourself to a greater experience of who you are. This takes courage. You will be stepping outside of your comfort zone. Even that is a choice.

It is a choice to be brave. It is a choice to face your fears. It is a choice to be in joy. It is a choice to express and experience love. It is a choice to be compassionate. It is a choice not to be in judgment of yourself.

It is your choice to honor and cherish the possibility of a magnificent destiny for a divine humankind. It is your choice to invite that possibility for yourself. It is your choice to step beyond the lethargy and the apathy and the fear and the absurdity of it all—the intimidating hugeness of it all—and to embrace it.

My advice? Choose it!

# *Lambs to Lions*

Envision yourself as a prisoner within a darkened cell. You have been imprisoned there for so long that you have even forgotten that your sight. But now you become aware that you have a device within your grasp that you had overlooked. In truth, you have been fearful of using it, because you have perceived it as a weapon.

This instrument is a laser. It is the laser of choice.

At first you fire wildly. Your choices are shot helter-skelter, rarely revealing any consistency. But eventually your choices begin to be more steady and focused on freeing yourself from your darkened prison. You begin to shatter through the thick walls of your cell—and light pours into your cell.

What a beautiful metaphor for the effects of *choice* upon one's life. Growth happens as a result of consciously choosing and then paying attention to what emerges from your choices—including your thoughts, feelings and emotions.

These choices will expand your experience of yourself. They will bring you joy and peace and comfort and a greater sense of who you are.

Initially, your choices may bring you dis-ease and discomfort. That is also fine. You are to pay attention to the feelings that arise from these choices also and forgive them. Do not judge them, do not fear them. Gently, quietly, let them go and then choose anew.

As you begin to discover the benefits of choosing well, you begin to hone the aim of your laser so that it fires with consistent intention. This enables more and more of the light of that which you truly are to shine upon your present conscious being.

You will continue to amplify this. You will continue to hone this laser. It is the laser of freedom.

*Choice* is the harbinger of *freedom*.

You will become better in your choices. You will become more confident in your choices. You will recognize that which your choosing accomplishes for you.

It frees you. It returns to you the power over your destiny. It returns you from the meek lamb into the lion that you are.

So without judgment, just choose. You need not fear crawling out of the comfort of your prison and into the world outside! How long can you continue to fear this? If you are forever just rocking cloistered in your corner, fearful of the unknowns beyond the walls, what manner of life are you leading?

Be gentle with yourself. Start with smaller choices. Overcome the fear. Face life in small measures at first, but face it.

And be aware! Have the awareness that you have the ability to crawl from your cage and leap off the precipice it is perched upon, down into the azure, cleansing waters like a dolphin arcing back into the sea.

There is great value in seeing others summon the courage and the faith to pick up their lasers. Great value in witnessing the results of their choices upon their beings and their lives. It brings the gift of being *aware* that it is possible. And this gift of *awareness* comes by way of having others to whom one can look upon, from whom one can gain a sense of confidence. "Ah, they have done it. Therefore I can do it too!"

This is the treasure brought by many great sages that have walked this earth. Much of what they have been has served one grand purpose, to demonstrate to the rest of humanity and to future generations,

*That which I am you are too. That which I do you can do and more. We are all children of God. Follow me not as sheep behind a shepherd, but as lions in the making. As cubs destined for their station in life and graced with the wisdom and guidance of their elders— showing them the way to realize their own greatness and magnificence.*

So as you choose like a laser, soon you will break through your walls, the light will emerge and you will become ever more confident in your choices and in your ability to choose.

Many, however, will not choose. Much of this is due to fear. It is also out of not knowing that they have choices, not recognizing that they have choices, that they are free to choose. And so they negate their abilities and do not honor themselves.

And remember always, there is never a wrong choice. So there is never a need to be in fear. That which we perceive to be right and wrong is simply a judgment within our own minds.

It is always just a matter of recognizing the choices that we have made and discovering whether those are choices we would wish to sustain and to make again.

There is no right or wrong.

What we might perceive to be a wrong choice is in fact a wonderful gift, because it serves to demonstrate to us that which we are not. It serves either to reflect to us that which we were and no longer find ourselves to be. Or it serves to ask us as we are stepping outside of ourselves, as we are stepping into new territory, as we are crossing our own boundaries, is this a direction we wish to take? And if not, so be it. No judgment. Gently, compassionately choose again.

We are brilliant creatures. We are divine and blessed. And if you acknowledge that truth, then your life will be led as if you are divine. This is tricky, for although you are already that, you may have to patiently remind yourself in order to believe it. The moment you doubt it, the moment you place worry upon your heart, doubt and fear, then life won't unfold as fluidly.

## The Playground

*Time stood still*
*As the two children gathered in their sandbox.*

*"Pick up your sword!"*
*She shouted and handed him the spade.*
*"You're a Princess!"*
*He laughed and placed the pail upon her head.*
*"I am Strong and Brave*
*And the Protector of this Kingdom!"*
*"And I am a Beautiful Ballerina!"*

*And they set to work building their castle,*
*Moats and turrets, courtyards and bridges.*
*And they took turns acting brave and dancing,*
*Being beautiful and strong.*

*How wonderful that it was all there*
*In the sandbox to begin with,*
*Just waiting for them to play.*

# *Expect Miracles*

As you walk the path of discovering your divinity, remember to be compassionate with yourself. Be gentle and forgiving. Nothing needs to be forced. Follow the flow.

This does not mean that you do not pay attention to your feelings. Many of you have lived your lives denying your true feelings and so it becomes a challenge for you to reconnect to yourselves. However, if you are honest with yourself, then you will know the truth of what you are feeling.

Courage will be required, because change often flies in the face of convention. Nothing is conventional about the process of setting your spirit free.

By understanding that your awareness in the past was more limited than your awareness of today—always as a result of gained experience—then you cannot fault yourself for past choices.

And if you determine that you made a *wrong* choice in the past knowing the possible repercussions, then forgive yourself for not having the courage then to make the *right* choice. For by not forgiving this, you adhere to the past and maintain an emotional tie to your prior choices. And this will cause your life to bring forth yet another experience to allow you to choose again, just so that you may confirm to yourself that the wisdom has been gained.

And again, remember that there is no right and wrong. Everything is simply what you choose it to be. So, if you choose to be happy, then you cannot make a choice that will bring unhappiness—if you are truly paying attention. If you choose to be secure, then you will have security but you may also have unhappiness. So be clear in your choices, be clear in your thinking, and pay attention to your feelings.

As you begin to practice this and have faith in the process and in yourself, it will become easier and you will notice the changes in your life. Expect miracles, because they will occur.

But do not be self-defeating. Do not say, "Ah, I want this..." and then proceed to choose poorly. Choose wisely. Pay attention.

And if ever you are unclear, then pause before you choose. Pause until you are clear. Then choose.

And if ever you choose and then find yourself uncomfortable with that choice, choose again!

It is like coming to a fork in a forest path. You head left because the scenery appears prettier but after a while you discover that it is not so. Simply turn around and take the other route. Neither path is right nor wrong, it is only what you choose to experience that matters.

# *Compassion*

As we choose to experience compassion for those around us, we will be drawn to those who are ready to reveal the truth of ourselves back to us. As we begin to forgive ourselves and experience compassion for ourselves, we free ourselves. We open ourselves to experience life more freely, without confines, without judgment.

Imagine, if you will, a woman who has led her life with such fear. Always walking on eggshells, having created so many rules about what is right and what is wrong. And who is constantly seeking outside of herself to define the rules of life.

Imagine—if you will—that in lifetimes past she was a prostitute ostracized by society and condemned. Imagine that she has lived lifetimes trying to repair that stigma. She has done this by trying to do what fits within the parameters of acceptable behavior. Yet this does not serve her because she has buried that one brilliant lifetime that has much wisdom to offer her—and that has much pain and judgment that has yet to be forgiven.

If she were to look beyond herself at those who fall outside the norms of patterned society, those who are brave and bold, different and adventuresome, she would reveal to herself the beginnings of wisdom. If she were to allow herself to experience compassion for those, to *understand* them, she would begin to look upon her own self with more compassion and freedom. And she would come to free herself of the self-imposed shackles from that distant memory.

Most of humanity fits into a mold. There are countless molds upon this planet. But ultimately we are meant to be a mold-less humanity. We are meant to define ourselves in the purity of the expression of that which we are in one moment—and of that which we choose to become in the next.

We shelter ourselves from the richness of our experiences when we reside in fear—when we have shunned a part of ourselves that is integral to the totality of that which we are. The path to discovering your divinity is the path of forgiveness and integration.

When this happens, when you truly release all of the judgments, express compassion for self, and bring to light that which was of you—which is very much integral to you—you then free yourself as a being, for you allow the depth of the experience to lend its wisdom to your totality. In essence, you become a greater, stronger and wiser kingdom. You free yourself to greater choice and greater expression, because you are no longer defined by things that are outside of you.

You bring everything within your heart. You bring to surface your fear. And through the healing power of forgiveness and understanding, you cease looking outward for signs of self-definition and of worthiness. For by bringing everything within your heart and truly, compassionately *understanding*, you can allow yourself to honor the wisdoms gained.

You align yourself to a greater awareness of yourself. And this then allows you to make choices that stem purely from the heart, that are based purely on your own wisdom, your own discernment, and your own knowledge. Then the opportunity for defining yourself becomes much more enlightened.

## *The Garden*

*Close your eyes and plant your feet firmly on the ground.*
*Take several deep breaths.*
*Picture yourself as a young tree in a beautiful meadow.*
*With each deep inhalation,*
*Allow your roots to be planted further into the soil.*
*With each great exhalation,*
*Experience yourself drawing up nourishment from the rich loam beneath.*
*Keep breathing and imagine yourself growing.*
*Your roots reach deeper and wider through the earth,*
*Stretching and stretching.*
*Notice as your trunk becomes thicker and more solid.*
*And your limbs begin to lengthen,*
*Stretching further into leaves that flap in the soft wind.*
*Inhale the beauty that is you—your fragrance, your magnificence.*
*Now look about you in the meadow and notice all who have assembled to witness your majesty.*
*The flowers that open their faces to you.*
*The brook that bubbles at your side.*
*The precious butterflies that flutter by.*
*The sun*
*The breeze*

*Enjoy this moment, immersed in this beautiful creation.*
*Now, free yourself of your tree-form.*
*Float from it gently.*
*And look about with your lighter, softer eyes.*
*Pay attention to what you see.*
*Pay attention to what you feel.*
*Pay attention to what you hear.*
*Witness nothing but love.*
*Witness nothing but joy.*
*Surrender yourself to this love.*
*Surrender yourself to this joy.*
*Know that this love and joy is ever present,*
*You need only visit this garden.*
*And so now with your heart full of love,*
*Your soul full of joy,*
*Gently depart this eden.*
*Slowly open your eyes.*

# Surrender Judgment

In our common human experience, we have judged good and bad, right and wrong. Instead of having amazing and unique life experiences and growing in wisdom, we have fragmented humankind and lapsed into judgment.

But in truth, we have only judged ourselves. These judgments of self have been so harsh and destructive that instead of holding them within, we have projected them outward onto others.

Think of it as energy. The resistance to release the energy of judgment causes it to build up. But the incapacity of the human system to retain so much heavy energy causes it to be thrust outward. The only judgment that has ever existed is self-judgment. But the very act of projecting that energy outward has made judgment of others a very real human experience.

We were meant to journey through this world as adventurers. It is our playground. We are here to experience all that there is to discover of ourselves—and by extension, of life. Remember, we have experienced every possibility within the realm of humankind's experience—oppressors and victims, paupers and royals, lovers and fiends. Our journey has been the construction of a magnificent pyramid rich with experience and wisdom.

And now in this grand era, the tides are turning. The rapid evolution of humanity and the planet is upon us. The energies that inhabit this plane are increasingly high and fine, embodying ever more pure and expansive frequencies and escalating us into the realm of enlightenment. In this remarkable age, the capacity for humanity to experience life here as fully conscious divine beings is emerging.

Humankind is an incredible, elaborate creation in-progress. We have been blessed with the ability to express the full spectrum of energies that I will define as *god-conscious individuality*. By this I mean the soul in form that is fully aware of his divinity and who expresses that in its fullness, yet through the individual experience and stream that is uniquely yours. This is the potential of all of humankind, and this potential has been seeded for activation in this season of global transformation that is now.

While it so happened that we did not remember our true nature, it was also very much intended that we rediscover it and bring the wealth of human experience into the capstone of our pyramid and enhance the wisdom of a conscious, divine human being.

We have witnessed great souls express this truth to us through the ages, ever reminding us of who we really are.

Those who were truly connected to the highest wisdom of the angelic realm pointed to a time when the meek would inherit the earth. This destiny referred to a time in the evolution of humanity when those who had discovered the path of love, the path of joy, the path of freedom and compassion and unity would transcend the lower vibrational experiences of duality, of fear—of fighting, oppression, limitation, force and separation—and emerge to inherit the world.

As one great master described it, we will be as children coming unto the Lord. It is through this innocence and trust, genuine joy and compassion, free of all our prior judgments and transparent to the world that we will come to know our own divinity.

All of this has been planned. It is the natural evolution of mankind since the time of Adam and Eve. Do you not see the signs in nature? As one great sage has reminded us, *As above, so below*. Well, he has further enlightened us to this truth, *As within, so without*. So can you now see how Mother Nature is simply reflecting the outward result of our inner transformation?

Just as we are shifting and growing, releasing our past judgments and deep-seeded fears, we can observe marked shifts in our physical bodies. Much of what we have held as stale negative energy has manifested as disease within our bodies. As we evolve in our consciousness, our bodies will naturally undergo a cleansing to release themselves of their built up toxins.

This cleansing serves another purpose, it readies the body to contain and express the higher, finer, more expanded frequencies that each will embrace in their individual expansion.

And just as this is occurring within our own individual beings, it is also occurring in our world. This is so because it has been designed for both the planet and humanity to commence its magnificent evolution in harmony. Even the planet is undergoing a series of cleansings that will rid itself of all its built up toxins and prepare it to be a realm of high vibrational consciousness.

So bless the evolution that is now upon us. Know that this has been heralded for time immemorial. And just as within our own beings our individual expansion may at times appear traumatic since we are discarding judgments and fears which have stifled us for eons, so too the cleansing of the planet may at times take on a very traumatic manifestation—earthquakes, hurricanes, avalanches, volcanic eruptions, tsunamis, droughts and floods.

But do not get drawn into the fear that such incidents have generally wrought. Know that these events will serve not only to cleanse our planet but also to bring many who experience them to reveal their deep-seeded fears and doubts.

We will see manifestations of humanity's remarkable transformation in everything from nature to politics, religion, business, education, family and culture.

Unity, compassion and truth will be the new hallmarks. Any organization that does not embody complete transparency at all levels will begin to face many challenges to its survival. Religion, government and business will undergo much change—in fact, this has already begun.

Allow this change to occur. Surrender deeply to this evolution. Trust that this is God's will. Be kind to yourself as the urge to grow besets you. For much patience and forgiveness will be required. But surrender it all to the light! Let go of all that is within you that no longer enriches you. Forgive all that you have judged, so that you too may be forgiven and cleansed in the season of our evolution.

And remember that there is nothing that needs define you but what you perceive yourself to be in your next moment. For ultimately, the only truths are love, peace and joy.

# Examining Life

You may find yourself reflecting on your past, reflecting on your choices. Looking at your regrets. And contemplating your choices. This can surely be a fine exercise to engage in. However I will ask you to remember this, you cannot judge your past. It does not serve you.

Each moment of your life is a new moment. And in each moment your life is created anew. Anything can manifest from the possibilities of that new life. Where you are now and where you choose to be is simply all that matters.

If you spend time regretting your decisions, then you dishonor yourself and you dishonor the miracle of this life that you've chosen to live. You see, your past is for the learning and the wisdom that you have gained. And the learning and the wisdom that you have gained are meant to teach you compassion. They are meant to give you the wisdom, compassion for self, compassion for others, compassion and understanding of life.

Therefore with open, objective, compassionate reflection, your present choices become more clear. But if your choices stem from a place of fear, then fear reigns.

*Ah, because I said this or did that; things did not work out, therefore I must be cautious and careful. Surely I cannot trust myself or others.*

This is a very common way of experiencing fear. If this is what ensues, then you have not learned appropriately. Your learning is hindered by judgment.

Non-judgmental learning, however, is simply to have observed yourself and your choices without judgment, thereby enabling yourself to be in a position to make better choices. And the better choices are simply those choices that enable you to achieve the goals that you have set upon for yourself in this life.

It's as simple as that—to realize your intentions.

Those who live without intentions become like sheep, being led wherever they may be led. Some are fortunate, some are not so fortunate, depending on which way the wind blows. But choice is critical to expanding and discovering your divinity. It truly is critical.

Not choosing is involution, stagnation which in times leads to devolution. Choosing is evolutionary.

And so now as you examine this in your life, your choices can be very clear. Abundance, love, mastery, joy, health and laughter. Without judgment of yourself. Without judgment of others.

Judgment is like the tightening of a belt. When the belt is too tight, energy cannot flow. Loosen the belt. Release your judgments. Gain the wisdom. Allow the energy to flow.

Be at peace.

Be at ease.

Have faith.

Call upon those that can help. Call upon the angels. Call upon your spirit guides.

And believe in unlimitedness. Believe in abundance. Because this belief defines you also. For you are unlimited and abundant. Allow everything to flow. Abundance in wisdom. Abundance in knowledge. Abundance in trust. Abundance in health. Abundance in wealth. Abundance in love. Abundance in laughter. Abundance in friendship. Abundance in impacting and expanding the lives of others.

And recognize how you may soar with the angels. Discard your old stories and embrace the new one. The one that tells you that you are magnificent and beautiful beyond your wildest imaginings.

## *His Bluff*

*While he sat atop his bluff overlooking the sea*
*And marveled at the waves as they crested and curled,*
*He wondered...*

*What if the ocean chose not to embrace its might and magnificence?*
*What if each droplet conceived of itself as idle and insignificant?*

*Where would all the surfers go?*

# *Terribly Wonderful Things*

Ultimately, we are all divine. It is this fundamental awareness—knowing that this is the truth of who we are—that propels our discovery of self. As we pay attention in our lives, we allow ourselves to reveal that which defines us.

Most people find it very difficult to accept their own individual magnificence. If you are truly divine—truly wise, brilliant, loving, compassionate, worthy of all abundance and fully aware of that same glorious divinity in all others—then you must accept that all that you have been, all that you have felt, thought and done, is part of that same magnificence.

But how can this be so? For deep within your being you know you hold harsh judgments. Consider your feelings for the liar, the thief, the abuser, the rapist and the slayer. Consider your feelings for all those in your midst who do not embody kindness, sincerity, fairness and consideration.

Everything that exists in this world is intimately connected to the totality of who you are. In your many life experiences, you have been each of these terribly wonderful things. It is only in your own minds that you judge them to be terrible. In truth, they are all wonderful. They all serve to enrich the individual—and humanity at large in—the knowledge of the full range of life experience upon this plane.

How is it that God may know in his infinite wisdom all that resides within the heart of mankind? Because he has entered each of these hearts and understood.

God is not the vengeful, judgmental, authoritarian deity that humankind has come to perceive. That is simply what God is understood to be from the perspective of the vast majority of humanity who have not yet opened their hearts to experience their own true nature. So the God they experience is simply a creation in their own image.

Your expansion into the full discovery of your divinity necessitates an embrace of all of mankind. For as you can begin to allow yourself to look upon others with compassion, then you open yourself to embracing yourself with compassion. And the truth of the depth of you is no less than you perceive the diversity of humanity to be.

Forgive yourself for your sadness, your grief, your loneliness, your anger, your frustration, your insensitivity, your recklessness, your misery, your suffering.

Can you genuinely perceive that you are as powerful and as magnificent as I say you are? For if this is so, then how is it that you could have said and done the things you have said and done in your life?

How is this possible if you are divine in nature? And if it is true, then how can you possibly be forgiven for having been so unconscious about your true nature? How can you right your wrongs and atone for all of your dark thoughts and unloving actions?

It is important to understand this primordial fear that many witness. You fear knowledge of your magnificence because it will lead you to look within and reveal to yourself everything that you are and have been that you would judge to be contrary to that magnificence.

Because you experience life within a paradigm of right and wrong, good and bad, your fear is the great fear of self-judgment, of self-condemnation. I am here to tell you that *judgment* is a man-made construct.

Judgment, as you have come to know it, has no bearing on your eternal soul or on the question of suffering God's wrath. There is no such thing as God's wrath. There is only God's love—and your resistance to know it.

So look within and allow all that you have judged in life to surface. For as you look within, these judgments will arise as secret judgments of self that you have held within your own heart. And these are now to be forgiven.

I will offer an illustration, an example that will help you to comprehend. Everyone's experience will be unique, but I am using this illustration to express how one may face an opportunity for expansion and transformation. I will speak to you here as if you are the subject of this example.

Let us assume that you are discovering a deep-seeded resentment towards those in your life who have held you down, restricted your freedom and silenced your voice.

I will start by reminding you that this has all been your own creation. Somewhere in time perhaps you had an experience that imprinted you with a fear of expressing your truth or your freedom.

Perhaps you were witness to the horrific slaying of a person dear to your heart, one who was outspoken and wise. This experience may have tragically shattered your faith in mankind resulting in lifetimes of fearing the result of your own freedom and outspokenness.

So now in your life of today, look beyond the frustration you have with those in your life who suppress you. Instead, bless them! For they are part of the brilliant orchestration of your own evolution.

At the level of your capstone, you have deemed yourself worthy of being free—and you have recognized your readiness. And so you have welcomed these frustrating relationships into your life to serve as triggers for moving beyond lifetimes of self-diminishment, triggers that will cause you to recognize that you have had enough of your fear.

As you look more honestly at your present experience of life, you come to see that you allowed these relationships to form and prevail. They were a comfort to you, providing you with the false sense of safety that you felt you needed.

This has all been your creation!

And as you now recognize that this is not who you choose to be anymore, that you wish to express your own truth, you wish to make your own choices in life, you wish to be free, then keep in the forefront of your mind that those with whom you have felt anger and resentment are not the oppressors you have deemed them to be.

They have simply carried out their roles in your brilliant play. You might even find that they have perceived their actions to be quite noble, caring for someone who they felt was incapable of caring for themselves. So be careful not to hold them in contempt.

Know that you will feel like a volcano ready to erupt as you go through this significant expansion. Because you have been suppressing yourself for so long, perhaps many lifetimes, your new sense of freedom will bring about a reaction to the many restricting forces and individuals you have knit into your life.

Situations will arise that will reflect to you the truth of who you have been, and you will feel a great energy rise within you that will express,

*No more! Do not talk down to me anymore! Do not suppress me any longer! Let me speak! Let me say what it is I have to say! Let me make up my own mind! Stop treating me with such disregard and disrespect!*

I will advise you to allow this volcano to erupt. The energy that will spew forth will cleanse your being of all the stale forces of self-diminishment and the self-imposed forces of fear that have defined you for so long. And as this energy clears itself from your being, much else that has attached itself to this dynamic will also be cleared. You will release yourself of much of that which no longer defines you.

Remember, others are not to be judged here in the same way that you are not to step into self-judgment and self-loathing for the lifetimes and lifetimes of such experiences that you have created for yourself.

Forgive yourself in the moment for all that has been. And recognize that this is not who you are anymore. Forgive yourself quickly and gently. And then allow yourself to change. It will take time, as there is much to cleanse from your being. But be patient.

So erupt as you must. You will find yourself reacting to your old situations and relationships. But do so peacefully, boldly and clearly. Say what must be said.

*I am not willing to be silenced anymore. I wish to make my choices for myself. Please don't treat me in such and such a manner.*

Be calm and clear and persistent. And allow the energy of your erupting volcano to be behind these words. For as much as you are demonstrating to the world that you are changed, more importantly you are reprogramming yourself in the new image of self you have discovered.

Remember that at this stage of your evolution, it is about you. So do not be too concerned with how others may respond to your changes, that is theirs to deal with—as long as you are careful not to lash out and descend into judgment of others for how they have treated you in your past. Be focused on your own magnificent discovery of self and continue to pay attention to your thoughts and feelings. Many of them will be new, so pay attention. And as I described, with your eruption will come a cleansing of more than you could have imagined.

Know also that this energy of transformation will act as the energy of propulsion, boosting you to even more grand discoveries of self. Forgive yourself quickly, judge neither yourself nor others, pay attention to your thoughts and feelings, trust that your capstone is guiding your course and you will find yourself in a remarkable spiral of ever-expanding brilliance. This is the path to discovering your divinity.

A remarkable thing will happen when you pay attention to the transformations in your life. Judgment ceases. As you recognize that you can easily and immediately forgive yourself for all your thoughts, feelings and behaviors that have reflected only insignificance back to you, then you are left in a state of surrender. A state of acceptance. A place of no judgment.

This is not an empty state. This is a state that is filled with trust and hope. And if you have seeded yourself with the awareness of what you truly are—a divine, blessed being—then you can begin to truly grasp what it is to be that divine human being.

You will realize that everything that you have been—regardless of how you may have perceived these in past judgments—is integral to the totality of you.

So your experiences as a tyrant, as a victim, as a beggar each are equally as important as your experiences as a lover, as a mystic and as a saint. And the same applies to your lifetimes as musicians, royalty, clergy, farmers, soldiers and prostitutes. Each has had its own wealth of experience that with open-hearted reflection can yield great wisdom.

This is the essence of our purpose in expansion—to integrate the multiplicity of all the we have experienced into a wholeness of self.

Imagine, if you will, a state of wholeness, wisdom and amusement at knowing the full spectrum of all of life's experience and having embraced your profound divine connection with both the source of all that is and every other life expression that exists. This state of being is the capstone of your pyramid.

Now imagine living your life with your unique personality and humanity intact but also in residence of your capstone. How remarkable would your life be? Is this not a worthy goal?

In this state, the full loving, compassionate, creative force that is you is seasoned with the wisdom of ages and experiences that transcend the finite. And you express as the magnificent divine being that you are, pursuing whatever creative impulses move through you and following a course in life that is consciously co-created between your divine capstone linked to source and the divine expression that is you in this lifetime.

This is your ultimate purpose for being.

This is the promise to humanity. This is the culmination of our common evolution. And this is the potential available to all in this remarkable age and time.

## *Forgive Me Father*

*Forgive me Father for I have sinned.*
*It has been a lifetime since my last confession.*

*I confess that I have not loved myself.*
*I confess that I not have seen myself to be*
*The noble being that you have told me I am.*
*I continue to doubt.*
*I continue to cast judgment on others*
*That truly is only a projection,*
*Only an extension of the judgment I hold of myself.*
*I continue to behave in a reactionary manner,*
*To not pay attention to what is truly happening*
*In every moment of my life,*
*To not use the sound judgment*
*That you have graced me with.*

*I continue to love in vain,*
*To love only for the less noble experience of human love,*
*That which brings only what my false ego knows*
*To be gratifying,*
*That props me in my stagnant position of today,*
*That fulfills the limitedness that I perceive myself to be,*
*But which pales in comparison to the truth*
*You tell me I am.*

*Soaring with Angels*

*I confess that though I may dip my toe*
*In the water of the divine,*
*I find it far easier to stay ashore,*
*To ignore the opportunity for expansion*
*That lies before me in every moment,*
*To revel in my dis-ease,*
*To muck about in the muck,*
*To excuse myself over and over and over again*
*For not choosing to be a better man,*
*A wiser man,*
*A more loving man.*

*I confess that I have seen the darkness*
*That resides within me,*
*The shadows of my being.*
*And these are comfortable to me.*
*I confess that though I may look upon them at times,*
*It is far easier to ignore and suppress them,*
*Than to face them directly and surrender them.*

*I confess that I look not too closely at my actions,*
*For to do so would cause me to question*
*Who I choose to be.*
*It would cause me to pause and ask,*

*Where from comes the wisdom,*
*Where from comes the strength*
*To be the man you have held me up to be?*
*And who is this man that I am to be?*

*I confess that I am not clear in my being,*
*That I still experience confusion and uncertainty.*
*I confess that I do not fully and truly know my path.*
*And though I wish to know it,*
*It is easier to rest in not knowing it.*
*For to know it would mean change.*
*And I confess that though I say I want change,*
*I do not often want to change.*

*I confess that I am attached to my personae.*
*I am attached to the image of me that I have created,*
*That I have shown to the world.*
*And I confess that I am comfortable within that image,*
*I do not wish to change it.*
*For to do so would compromise me*
*In the eyes of those around me,*
*Would make me appear weak.*
*And I confess that weakness is not something*
*I hold in esteem.*

*Father I confess that I am a hypocrite.*
*I confess that I will say that I am fine*
*When in truth I am not fine.*
*I will say that all is well*
*When truly all is not well.*
*I will say that I am happy*
*When in truth I am sad.*

*I confess that my life is one competition after another.*
*I am competing for survival.*
*I am competing for love.*
*I am competing for success.*
*I am competing for attention.*
*I am competing to be wiser and brighter and smarter and faster and better than everyone else.*
*I am competing to be right.*
*I am competing to be in control.*

*And, oh dear Father,*
*I confess that though I do challenge myself,*
*Though I seek your forgiveness,*
*I truly do not embrace that forgiveness within me.*
*I continue to feel empty and unloved.*
*Unworthy.*

*And that continues to make me feel sad*
*And angry*
*And distant.*
*Separate.*
*It continues to cause my life to be discordant.*
*Insecure and unstaid.*
*It continues to make my days stressful,*
*My moments peppered with fear.*

*I confess that though I say I love you*
*And I love those around me,*
*I do not often experience that love.*
*Nor do I express it.*
*I confess that though I see those rare few*
*Who experience life differently,*
*Magically and abundantly,*
*I do not trust them.*
*I do not trust that they live this in truth,*
*That they experience this in truth,*
*That they are this in truth.*
*For how can this be possible?*
*They must surely be in denial.*
*For life is hard.*
*Life is a struggle.*

*No one can master such dominion over themselves,*
*Over their thoughts and their fears.*

*I confess that I believe that only a sainted one,*
*A blessed special seed of the divine,*
*Can be so noble and so magnificent.*
*For if it were not so,*
*Then surely I am no different from them.*
*But that cannot be so.*
*For I am not like them.*

*I confess that I do not believe*
*That it is simply my awareness,*
*My choices,*
*That make me different from those most noble of beings,*
*Those most noble of women and of men*
*Who have walked upon this earth and have been divine,*
*Blessed,*
*Joyful, creative, purposeful,*
*Loving beings.*
*I confess that though I am drawn to this notion of being*
*Divine,*
*Though it inspires me,*
*I truly do not believe it of me.*

*Oh my dear Father,*
*I am collapsed on my knees.*
*My head is in my hands.*
*Protect me and save me from myself,*
*For my demons obscure my sight and make cold my heart.*

*Oh my dear Father,*
*I beseech you to look upon me.*
*Show me your light that I may be comforted,*
*That I may be guided to be drawn nearer.*

*Oh my dear Father,*
*Help me to surrender all of my loneliness,*
*All of my sadness,*
*My regrets*
*And my fears.*
*Take from me my doubts*
*And my judgments.*
*Cleanse me of my unworthiness.*

*Oh my dear Father,*
*If you would only show me the way,*
*If you would only show me how,*
*I would move mountains to bathe in your light.*

*Oh my dear Father,*
*Know that I love you deeply.*
*If I could but know you as deeply,*
*I would be complete.*

*Oh my dear Father,*
*Please bless me and hold me close to your heart,*
*That I may truly know your heart and so truly be blessed.*

*Oh my dear Father,*
*Let me be forever and ever in your kingdom of divine blessed glory.*
*Amen.*

## Our Inheritance

Can this all possibly be true? To be divine? That you are divine? That this is a unique time in the history of humanity?

You have lived so long within the confines of your limited reality, how is it that you can accept that all this is real? How is it that this transformation of which we speak can be possible?

Human experience is and always has been one of free will. And humanity has chosen all over the spectrum of possible experiences. We have been saints and sinners, paupers and kings, idle and passionate. We have done it all and been it all.

But now in this season of evolution, of grand transformation, the experience of the world as you know it is shifting into the world of magic, the opportunity to break free of the cloistered experiences of your past into the brilliant experiences that await, the experiences of heaven on earth, of man living as gods. This opportunity is one you simply cannot avoid facing. And as it rears itself from within your very being to be faced, it is for you to choose.

And we have wisely seeded our lands with way showers, forerunners, those who have achieved mastery, awakened from their common slumber, crossed the river into their magnificence.

And they are teachers only insofar as they may teach you what they themselves learned. How it was that they found the river. How they summoned the courage to cross it. What demons emerged to be quelled forever. And how this was done.

I say to you, *Believe!* Believe. Seek out those who have begun to shine, those who reveal the very essence of love and truth, wisdom and compassion, magnificence and abundance, joy and glory. Seek them out for they have much to tell you. Much guidance to offer. Much love and encouragement to give. They will help you see more clearly when your fears arise to distract you from your resolve.

Let them teach you how to trust yourself. For this is not meant to be an exercise in surrendering your judgment to the judgment of others. This is meant to be a time to expand your awareness to a realm beyond judgment so that you are individually connected to the all knowing, compassionate and merciful godhead of your being.

This is the part of you that is the capstone of your unique individual divine being. It is the part of you that knows you intimately and loves you absolutely. It is the part of you that knows your experiences and knows your heart and knows your mind completely. It is the part of you that has only compassion for you. It does not—and cannot—judge you. For there is nothing to judge. There never was anything to judge.

It is the part of you that expresses the same divine love as God—and so it knows with complete understanding that everything you have been and done, everything that you have said and thought, every act, every feeling was what it was in the moment. It was part of the experience of you in that very moment of that very experience. And it is part of the incredible and intricate tapestry that enriches you.

So I encourage you to learn how to connect to your own divine capstone, your own source of truth and discernment. Allow your guidance to flow from within, resolute in the ever-expanding knowing that you are ultimately your own greatest guide.

Now is the time of our inheritance. Humanity is receiving the promise that is seeded within us all. The promise of heaven. The promise of Eden. The promise of magnificence and joy, love and fulfillment. Now is the time for this brilliant unfolding.

*See through divine eyes.*
*Allow yourself to soften your gaze and smile.*
*And see truly through divine eyes.*
*Let the practice train you.*
*Let the practice be a constant remembering of who you are.*
*Look about you with compassion at all times,*
*With grace at all times,*
*Recognizing the divinity in all—at all times.*
*For when you do this, you cannot forget your own divinity.*

# Improving My Game

As I began making a regular practice of paying attention to my feelings, I was amazed at what began to surface. I began to notice how in my seemingly quiet days I would experience resentment and loneliness, sadness and frustration. I would feel misunderstood and disregarded, bitter and upset. I would feel alone and unsupported.

It was a while before I sifted through these heavy emotions. Truth be told—the hardest thing was to be honest with myself about what it is I was really experiencing. It was so much easier to blame others for making me feel a certain way.

I'd blame others, I'd blame life, I'd blame my upbringing. And I would be genuinely crestfallen when I would be guided to look within for the reason for my frustrations.

How could it be? It made perfect sense that because *she* was dishonest or because *he* was controlling that I was reacting as I was. That I was feeling as I was. That I was powerless as I was.

How maddening that I was being guided to accept that although my observations may be very valid, they had no real bearing on my feelings or my reactions!

Ah, but I persisted. Know that I have a deep and abiding faith in the divine guidance I have in my life. I know it to be a grace and a precious gift not to be dismissed, not to be overlooked and not to be trifled with.

So with the greatest of kind and gentle—yet firm—guidance, I allowed these feelings, many of them reactions, to surface.

For much of my life I have had a very strong sense of my energy centers in my physical and etheric body. I have been aware of the frequencies associated with the divine wisdom that graces my life.

And I have been aware of the energies affecting my solar plexus. For many years, this particular region served as a divining rod for me to gauge my world. I have been able to sense the veracity of others, their intentions, their state of mind—in fact, their state of being. I have been able to gain a quick sense of the dynamics of a situation. The safety of a space or a course of action.

As I refined my senses, I was even able to read an article or hear a word or a name and gauge the energy associated with it—I've been able to sense whether there was something there for me to explore and pursue or if I was approaching a dead end. And this remarkable disk—for I experience the solar plexus chakra as a brilliant disk that can spin on its axes—would also generate an uncomfortable sensation in my belly when there was an emotion that arose that was steeped in a past experience, a past life or a distorted belief of mine.

Many times it was difficult for me to discern between what was mine to examine and what was being experienced of another that I was encountering. And since so many of my experiences occur through interactions with others in my life, this became a tricky thing to navigate. I had vested so much in the subtle experiences to reveal truth to me, and I was paying very close attention to my experiences in an effort to grow spiritually. Yet all of a sudden some were becoming difficult to interpret.

I remember a couple of significant experiences in my life that were impacting the very course I would be taking in life—a new business, a new relationship. And I was relying on what I have always been led to honor, my own personal divine guidance. And my guidance system was failing me! At least that's how I experienced it at the time.

In hindsight, I can say that it was only a matter of having to improve my game. I had never dug so deeply before to uproot the deep-seeded elements of my own self that required cleansing and enlightenment in order to enable me to step closer to the conscious divine experience I was choosing for. But now that I was doing this important work, I needed to draw upon even more evolved skills of discernment to be able to reveal truth to myself.

And so I was guided to incorporate my intellect. At first this was a foreign thought to me. *Intellect is the enemy! It's the proponent of the false ego! It sustains and maintains beliefs of old in order to validate and justify a limiting life. It's not to be trusted!*

But this was not true. I came to realize that the intellect only inhibits our growth when we do not use it with an open heart. With courage and determination. With a clear and willing intention to set aside all common beliefs that have only brought us to today and to explore possibilities that can move us towards our goal.

I admit that it was very refreshing to be given this new perspective. For the highest of truth is that while I know myself to be steeped in matters of the heart—divine love, compassion and forgiveness—I am truly one who has always enjoyed the brilliant machinations of a sharp intellect.

So my intellect became another tool in my arsenal of discernment. And when I would experience a reaction to an experience, I would candidly ask myself if there was any logical reason for me to feel what I was feeling under the circumstances.

It became a brilliantly simple practice. But it required utter honesty, complete truthfulness, what I like to refer to as *absolute transparency* with myself.

In so doing, I would discover what was mine to examine more closely and what was not mine. Oftentimes what was not mine required no further action or response on my part. I could simply let it go. If intense, I would shake myself of the remnant emotion by reconnecting with my divinity in a number of different ways.

One thing that I did come to discover in time was that the intense emotions were deeply-rooted beliefs that required adjustment. They were important to look at and cleanse.

What I discovered to be mine to examine more closely would receive priority in my life. It was as if I would place it on a silver platter in front of my face so that it could neither be forgotten nor denied and so that it would be looked upon as the gift that it was—a gift to cleanse, a gift to heal, a gift to expand me more fully into the truth that I am. The truth that we all are.

As you undertake this same commitment to self examination, you will find that your judgments will be replaced with feelings of understanding and compassion. You will come to understand that your denials of past have in truth simply been an inability and a fear to look within and discover the truth of who you are.

Fundamentally that's the truth of this all. Why do you continue experiencing what you do? The answer is very basic. Because that's what you draw to yourself. You haven't known any differently. The notion that you bring everything upon yourself is at first a hard notion to grasp. But it's the truth.

With compassion, judgment loses its hold. Judgment of self and judgment of others. Judgment is replaced with understanding. It is replaced with the wisdom to allow others to be whoever they choose to be.

What a powerful gift to not hold people in contempt for being who they are! For not judging them! For allowing them to be who they choose to be. Doing so does not diminish your divinity. Nor does it prevent them from recognizing the divinity that they are. But if this is not where they are in their journey, then what a powerful gift to simply allow them their path!

As you embrace this bit of wisdom, you will notice a great shift within your own being. For as easily as you can surrender your judgment of others and simply allow, you will discover your freedom to just as easily surrender your judgments of self. And from this place of being, your growth and your expansion in discovering your divinity will be rapid.

If our focus in life were to shift from an outward focus—worship or judgment—to an inward focus on self discovery, the divine birthright of humanity would be realized. Love and abundance and peace and joy. We would no longer be a civilization struggling in fear and limitation, struggling for power and control. We would be a peaceful, creative society enjoying the magnificence of a divinely conscious life in a wonderfully magical world.

## Solitaire

*Who are we that we seek expression?*
*And who are we to express magnificence?*

*Can we revel in the brilliance of our unique individuality*
*While also embracing that same brilliance in all?*

*And can we possibly be subtly amused*
*By the mundane intricacies of this world*
*While passionately entrenched in the miracles of life?*

*Ponder this while you pretend to play solitaire.*

# The Blanket

I do not believe that now is the time for monastic pursuits. You are all divine beings having a human experience. You are not meant to deny your humanity. You are not meant to deny your worldly engagements. You are not meant to surrender the physical. In fact, especially in this magnificent space-time that is now, that is the enlightenment of the planet and her inhabitants, it is ever more imperative that you stay fully present within your physical beings and within your life experiences so that you may expand with all aspects of this reality intact.

It is the time to fully embrace the totality of your unique self and your life experiences, cleansing yourself to crystalline perfection so that you may expand to incorporate the higher finer vibrations of wisdom, love and healing that are pouring into our world at this time.

Now is the time to integrate your past. Now is the time for courage and faith. These two elements are what each of you must call upon in every moment as you face the deepest hidden emotions that must surface to be surrendered and cleansed. These are the cancers within your being. These are the fats that weigh you down. These are the dark unknown memories that limit your experience and your expression of truth. These are the ugly bits of your many lifetimes that have been judged and suppressed and denied.

After all, how can a brilliantly crafted bell ring its most beautiful tone for the world to hear when it is encrusted in crud?

The cleansing is nothing more than allowing. It is allowing the feelings that you cannot comprehend, that cause you great fear, that resonate within your being as discomfort and disease. It is allowing these to come up for each of you. And as they come up, you must remember to breathe. You must remember the truth of who you are.

You must remember that darkness is not a force by itself. It is not a presence to be feared. Darkness is merely the absence of Light. And so by allowing these things to surface, you allow light to be shed upon them. And you do so in places of love and wisdom, with those around you who embody the truth and support the light.

And you shall walk through the valley of the shadow of death—for that is how it may feel. But you shall remain faithful and trusting in knowing that you do this with divine intent and surrounded by the glory of God's will.

For the will of God I speak of is *to know God*. And you are all gods seeking to know yourselves.

How difficult is it to comprehend that you have been made in the likeness of God? God is Love, God is Truth, God is the Creator of all things. And so are you. All things.

You are even the creator of humankind's limited, dense reality of duality and separation, this suffering that so many have described as the foundation of human experience. But it is not that. Suffering is no different from darkness. Suffering is the absence of Light.

In essence and in truth, you are all Light. You are all gods. How can it be otherwise? If God is all things, then you too are God. And the more you permit yourself to accept that, to fully surrender to the reality of that Truth, then you can begin upon the path of self discovery. It is the ego that denies this reality. It is the ego that will place this possibility outside the realm of human engagement. It is the ego that relegates this Truth to but a few.

And this ego of which I speak is nothing more than your comfortable, centuries-old limiting beliefs. They have become like a warm blanket that comforts you in your slumber. You have become like the depressed man who sleeps through his life for fear of facing his day and casting judgment upon himself, for fear of discovering that what he has known and who has been is not the highest Truth. For fear of surrendering his false pride to possibly be shown something more magnificent.

But you must do this! You must summon courage from the very depths of your being and lift yourself from your slumber of comfortable beliefs, the ones that remove all responsibility for your own divine discovery from you and place it outside yourself. Drop this blanket! Face the cold morning and seek with earnest intent to have Truth revealed to yourself swiftly and lucidly.

## *Tis time*

*Gently close your eyes*
*Take several deep breaths*

*With each inhalation expand your belly*
*Draw in as much fresh air as your body will allow*

*With each exhalation*
*Surrender*
*Unclench your jaw*
*Let loose*

*With each inhalation*
*Know that you are also imbibing brilliant light*
*High fine frequencies of love*

*With each exhalation*
*Release all old stale energies within your being*
*That no longer enrich you*
*That no longer serve you*
*That no longer enliven you*
*Let them go*

## Soaring with Angels

*Know that you have buried yourself*
*Deep within a closet for a very long time*

*This closet is safe and it is warm*
*But it is also dark*
*Very dark*

*It is like a closet within a closet*
*Deeply recessed*

*Picture yourself hiding behind*
*The old coats*
*The hanging scarves*
*You have been all alone*

*And as you continue to breathe*
*Imagine yourself beginning to fill up with light*
*The very cells of your body take in this love*
*They begin to glow*

*Someone has opened the doors and is beckoning you*

*It is time to lay down your blanket*
*To open your eyes*
*To venture out into the light*

*It is time to summon your courage*
*To draw on your faith*
*To know all will be well*

*It is time to trust*
*That light brings with it only goodness and love*
*Kindness and learning*
*Healing and strength*

*It is time to be free*

## *A Greater Understanding*

Much of humanity's experience is that you cannot perceive of yourself as being magnificent because you have been taught for so long that you are sinful. To express humility—true humility—is not a possibility for you. It is perceived to be the greatest sin. To equate yourself with God is blasphemous. And yet that's exactly what you are. The truth is that the notion of any separation from God is the only sin!

Divinity is universal. It is underlying in all. The current global human consciousness does not embrace this reality. The fiction that most experience is something that each of you has individually accepted. But the time for experiencing insignificance is ending.

Now is the time to embrace the reality that you are all beautiful. At least begin to know your magnificence, to begin to experience this truth. It will take time and effort to *become* that knowing. There's shedding to be done, perceptions to be released. You will be not only creating a new understanding of yourself but also disposing of the unholy, un-whole perceptions of yourself.

For many of you who have begun to uncover your brilliance, it has been a painful process. This is so because some of your beliefs have been worn like clothing. They have blanketed you and made up your identity and your sense of security. And so the release of these has rendered feelings of betrayal and loss.

But today it need not be so painful nor so difficult. The structures from outside that hold the old realities in place—that define and confine and constrict—are not so firm. They are not so rigid anymore. The lightness of our time makes it so.

The energies of the planet have shifted. You are being bombarded by those same energies that are forcing an awakening. They are shattering the lower energies of consciousness and bringing forward enlightened consciousness. This has impacted you on many, many levels and you have begun seeing the effects in society—in politics, religion, education, and business.

Rigidity is crumbling. That which does not serve the greater good is crumbling. That which is not resonant with Truth is crumbling. That which does not support the expansion of the consciousness of humanity is crumbling.

Transparency is what is bringing forward more understanding. Secrets have no place in our times.

The work that you will do is not for the faint of heart. It will bring up all of that which is within you—the emotions, the memories, the fears—bring everything up and out. For this is what it is to cleanse the heart. It is to cleanse the entirety of your being.

How is it that you can take this concretized heart that most of humanity has and shatter it? Is there not some chipping required at times? The hammer may be hard, but the hand which swings it is golden with love.

What will be called for is honesty. And so for those of you who pursue this work, summon your faith, your trust and your courage. And believe that you will emerge truly cleansed.

Believe that the result of your cleansing shall be joyful, peaceful, abundant splendor and magnificence. Your noble efforts will reveal you to be a magical, enlightened, wise and loving being.

You will walk knowing who you are. Knowing your grace. Knowing your divinity. Your very presence will heal and teach others. It will demonstrate to them the truth that has been so elusive for so long—what it is to be the god-in-woman, the god-in-man that you are.

## *Know*

*Breathe deeply,*
*And know who you are.*
*Yes, everything is about to change.*
*All your petty human troubles will dissipate.*
*You may put them behind you.*
*And if they reappear, forgive them in that very moment.*
*Not only forgive, but forget in that moment—do not dwell.*
*Know so solidly who you are that nothing disturbs you.*
*Nothing moves you from that knowing.*
*Surrender your attachment to feeling wronged.*
*For it simply is not real anymore.*
*You have pretended that you can be offended.*
*You have pretended that you can be wronged.*
*You have pretended that you can be scorned.*
*You cannot!*
*This is what is changing.*
*This is part of your evolution, the unveiling of your sacred heart.*
*This is part of the integration of your divine self.*
*So breathe deeply.*
*Know who you are.*

# Time to Be Real

What good are your beliefs?

Most of you are guided by your social and religious attitudes. But what good is any of this to you? It is as if you are wearing a mask. A costume that proves you to be something you are not. It shows you to be experiencing something you are not. It is a portrait of laughter where there are tears. Am I not correct?

Has it not been given, as above so below? And does it not follow, as within so without? So if one experiences true inner peace without conflict, then would this not necessarily be reflected in one's outward life experiences?

You must remain ever truthful at this level of inner work. You must be courageous and willing to face and understand your fears. Have faith! Trust! Know that the clouds will part, that the heavens will pour down on you all that you are worthy of having and experiencing and being!

And if you cleanse yourself, if you move ever sure-footed towards clearing and expanding yourself, then why should your experiences not lead you to freedom? The only reason they would not is if there is within you yet an unresolved experience of needing to have suffering, needing to punish yourself, needing to be judged, needing to do anything to be unworthy of returning to God.

Can you take the leap of faith that is required and accept that you are indeed worthy? That you have always been worthy? That there is nothing within the realm of human experience that can possibly separate you from being the god that you are? That there is nothing within all of reality that causes you ever to be separated from God? From Love? From Truth?

There is no need for suffering. There is no punishment. There is no retribution. There never was a separation from God and there never will be a separation. It is only in your own minds, in your own limited beliefs and your own experiences in the moment.

So wake up! Wake up! Be your own truth. What is there to fear? What are you so attached to that you would not risk for the sake of truth, for the sake of discovery, for the sake of peace and love and strength and your own well-being?

And if you are so attached to your things and to your beliefs, then know that this is what it is that you fear compromising in this moment. Know it and own that knowing.

You can make decisions based on fear, but what a life that will be. It is the life that most of humanity has already created. Are you not yet tired of it? Has the result not yet proven to you that it is empty and devoid of inspiration?

Or you can be truly free and be completely unattached. This does not mean that you will not be fully engaged in life and in the enjoyment of your experiences. It means that you will have no fear-based attachments. It means your life can become a pure experience in the moment, of the moment—in every moment.

What is it that you have to fear anyway? Yes, many of you have had lifetimes of punishment, of judgment and of condemnation. So be it. Forgive that. For if you do not, you allow that darkness to have eminence in your life. You allow ignorance to prevail.

Is this still what you wish to allow? Or is there a new way? Is there a cleansing within your own being that may allow your life to be so gilded with love that though many may still judge it, condemn it and spit upon it, they will never ever diminish it? For within your own being you will have claimed and acknowledged the truth of your own vast experience. You will have made peace with your own past limited experiences and your own past judgments—and you will have resolved these. No external judgments will ever again trump this knowing.

So there is no need any more to judge yourself or others. Have only compassion. And be in understanding of those who still reside within the space of their limited experiences. For you have done this too.

Love is the only experience that need remain. Not the airy fairy love that humanity has perceived love to be. The love I speak of is far, far greater than this.

Choose for this. Hunger for this. Ask for this. For it is true, that which you ask for you shall receive. But know that for you to be ready to receive the magnitude of love's splendor that is your legacy, you must become like the handcrafted flute hewn from ancient bones and seasoned through the labor of self-perfection—open to receive the heavenly breath of love and express it as the unique, brilliant music that will be your words, your deeds and your creations.

## *The Nameless*

*It is the subtle experience of one recognizing another,*
*The act of the namas te.*
*It is that subtle field of awareness,*
*The Love,*
*The life-force itself,*
*That resides around us,*
*That surrounds us.*
*You recognize this powerful force.*
*It is love.*
*It is creation.*
*It is a conscious Consciousness that stimulates the consciousness of life.*
*It is love and light.*
*And it penetrates darkness and ignorance.*
*It is the creative force that penetrates slumber.*
*It is powerful.*

# The Path to Discovery

There is a great sense of understanding and compassion when you connect with the highest realms of spirit. There is an offering of wisdom that is both personal to your individual life path as well as general in its relevance to humanity at large.

This engagement with the teachings and the love of the higher realms necessarily brings with it an uplifting force. So it will inspire you with the divine force of upward movement to an ever higher and finer level of consciousness.

Many may be unaware that this is happening, but this in truth is the natural effect of such engagements. For as you embrace this wisdom, as you seek out the guidance, and as you hunger for a greater and more expansive awareness of yourself and of life, this is the natural outcome.

These energies will work as a whirlwind to stir up any debris from the lowest realms of your consciousness and bring them to the surface of your present-moment experience for cleansing, for forgiving, for enlightenment. You will be shedding light upon those aspects of your experience which have been hidden in the darkness out of fear or shame, resentment or anger, for whatever reason that may have caused you to suppress or deny them.

In order to step more fully into the light, you must bring your full self into the light of consciousness.

This means that all aspects of your greater experience or any knowing or belief that is not resonant with Truth, Love and Compassion—that is not in harmony with the grander consciousness to which we are all compelled—these will surface in order to be noticed again and experienced anew, addressed and resolved.

So it is no surprise that those embracing this path oftentimes find themselves facing darkness and often experience this as demons outside of themselves. In truth they are not. They are merely those aspects within your being that are now ready to surface and be healed.

So the guidance I would offer here is do not turn away from facing your demons. Do not fear the emotions that surface, no matter how dark and foreboding, fearful and destructive they may appear. Seek to uncover them so that you may begin to cleanse yourself of these malignant aspects and deliver unto them the light.

For when light is cast upon shadows, things are seen differently. Things are experienced differently. And nothing is anymore hidden from reality. You will allow yourself to forgive yourself these things so that what remains is the wisdom of experience of this darkness without the fear associated with it.

Heed these words. It is not simply for you to divorce yourself of your past insignificance, your past unconsciousness, your past darkness. It is for you to embrace these anew by bringing light into these dark recesses and allowing yourself to look upon these pasts with compassion and understanding. With the compassion of a mother who loves her child fully at all times. With the understanding of a man who looks upon his youthful pursuits with an awareness and a quiet wisdom that what was, was. With the fundamental knowing that everything that has been makes up the greater experience of what is here and now.

So do not attempt to deny any aspect of the greater self that makes up the multiplicity of your vast experience. Embrace these and forgive them. Allow them to be healed within your being, to be lightened. And integrate them into the grander awareness you have chosen to expand into.

After all, what do you think it is within me that enables me to look into the eyes of a sinner and see a saint? It is simply that I have been that sinner and I now know myself to be a saint—and this without denying that I have experienced what it is to *not* be a saint!

For you who step onto this path and then find yourself resisting your inner work, be forewarned. Your path will not be easy. This path calls for you to examine yourself and your lives in order to embrace yourself more fully. You will need to forgive yourself and others for your hard experiences. You will come to reconstruct your beliefs to enable you to embrace the truth of who you are.

These things are truly very simple. But they are not so easy.

Know that your deepest, darkest fears and limited beliefs will be stirred and they will surface in your life. Life will bring you examples of your shadows from the world around you. And you will be called upon to pay attention! For if you do not pay attention, the darkness will grow until you find yourself so uncomfortable within your reality that you are compelled to look again. For ultimately everything that you experience in your world is always just a reflection of your inner experience of self.

Be wary and do not blame *life*. For although I may write that *life will bring* your lessons, in truth it is *you that brings* these things to yourself.

It is the law of attraction. Everyone seeks to master it, but few understand its true import and measure. The law of attraction applies to things of the material plane only as an extension of the core process at work within.

In essence, the law of attraction is the law of energy, of resonance, of magnetism, and of consciousness. So if you are operating without integrity, this will be your experience and your attraction. And you cannot fake your way out of this. It is not *pretend and project* that will overrule the workings of this law. This law works with Truth.

Know that it matters not how you may be perceived by others—many of you work so hard to present yourself to the world in a particular way in order to be received by the world in that way—well this has no currency in the world of Truth and in the result of your experience of yourself in your world. Unless you are also deceiving yourself, your experiences will not shift to a more expanded or enlightened place just by projecting that reality. Work must be done.

Remember always that light attracts light. So remain forever focused on the one Truth that matters, your divinity. Stay true to your choice for expansion. Hold firm to your desire to embrace fully your divinity.

Trust that every experience you have as you step forward on your path only serves to bring you ever closer to *being* the divine, blessed angel you are. By doing this, your path will be easier and you will know that however difficult things may become, the light at the end of you tunnel will dazzle you and fill you with treasures beyond your imagining.

## *Warrior*

*Oh Noble Warrior,*

*Lower your shield,*
*There is no more need for defenses.*
*Lay down your armor,*
*The steel of this world is faded.*
*Discard your breastplate,*
*May your heart expand beyond its cinches.*
*Cast off your helmet,*
*That your voice and your truth may be known.*
*Soften your stance,*
*That others may see it is wise to soften theirs.*
*Surrender your sword,*
*The battle is done.*

*Oh Most Noble Warrior!*

*The great love of your mother seeks to embrace you,*
*The great love of your father seeks to embolden you.*

# Seek Further

As you raise your vibration, there is a most sublime experience of peace and joy and deep satisfaction that overcomes you. This can be both intoxicating and enticing. Many have chosen to make this their life purpose, to merge forever in this ocean of sublime delight.

It is beautiful, to be sure. But I will ask you to seek further. Seek to identify the qualities of the essence to which you connect. Seek to know these and to feel their presence in your life.

It is one thing to float away into the realm of the unseen and the sublime and to satisfy yourself that you have gained enlightenment and wisdom. To rest as your perception shifts to viewing your world differently and tapping into wisdom from on high for others. But I caution you to continue to pay attention. Pay attention to your thoughts. Pay attention to your feelings. For you may begin to experience a vacillation.

You may notice that while you immerse yourself in the ethers everything is magical and blissful, yet when you return to your mundane life there are feelings of emptiness and sadness that linger. These are real. These are pointing you to as yet unresolved patterns and memories that are still part of your being. This is where great courage and great leaps of faith are needed to allow these feelings to emerge.

Do not resist these notions any further. Do not push them away as if they are the distraction from your greater course. Face them. Allow them to surface. Feel fully what you are feeling, what you have been denying, what you have been avoiding. And as you allow these feelings to surface, know that the only release is forgiveness.

Your loneliness may reveal sadness. Your sadness may reveal regret. Your regret may reveal bitterness. Your bitterness may reveal anger. Each of these emotions is a powerful energy pattern that is a real part of yourself. So each one must be brought to surface.

And as you allow these emotions to come forth, there will be all manner of events that coincide in your life—both big and small—that will enable you to feel these emotions afresh. These experiences will act as triggers to heal past unresolved experiences.

So pay attention to these experiences. And feel your truth fully. Do not judge the experience as unholy or unworthy of your perceived state of awareness. This is not beneficial to your greater unfolding. Honor these experiences and the reactions they trigger within your being.

I would not condone acting out with aggression and violence. This is not what it means to honor your feelings. But I would encourage expressing your truth in all moments. Do not be concerned about the impact of your expression on others. For others will have been drawn to this experience for their own learning too. And do not sit in judgment as to why others may have been drawn. In your quiet moments, simply bless them for being a party to your own unfolding.

These experiences that you bring unto yourself may be quite uncomfortable. I say to you, do not shrink. Do not resist. Do not find ways to con yourself out of engaging them in truth. Step into them.

Face them as a skydiver faces his first jump. Face the resistance, face the trepidation, face the fear. And trust your readiness, trust your conviction, trust your parachute. And jump!

## *Imaginings*

*Imagine a world of laughter and sunshine*
*Children running about in gleeful abandon*
*Sweet air*
*Kind souls*
*Outstretched arms*

*Now open your eyes*

*Possibilities lie in the moment of your imaginings*

## *Do You Believe?*

Do you believe in Angels? I mean, really believe? That they exist? That they are wise? That they love mankind? That they make themselves and their love and their wisdom known to mankind?

Do you believe the stories of those who have seen angels appear to them in their life? Those who have received messages of inspiration and comfort in their times of need?

Do you believe that the prophets of old actually encountered angels in their very midst who brought with them messages from God? Do you believe this is true?

Do you believe that *you* can be so noble as to commune with the angels?

Be emboldened by Michael?

Be challenged by Uriel?

Be enraptured by Raphael?

Do you believe that the angels would take such an interest in you as to offer their solicited guidance and wisdom to aid you in negotiating the twists and the turns of your own unique path in life?

Do you believe that the angels would hear your prayers, that they would wake you from your coma, that they would shine their light upon doors they wish you to open?

Do you believe the angels would wish for you to discover as much of your divinity as you can possibly embrace so that they may celebrate the awakening of another sister, another brother into the realm of magnificent creator?

Well, why not?

Angels are a part of the greater reality that is ours. Not to recognize them is simply ignorance. Take no offence. By *ignorance* I mean *not knowing*, nothing any more sinister than that.

When I tell people that they can commune with the angels, there's often disbelief.

*How can that be? How is that an average person can be worthy of speaking with the Angels?*

Yet this is exactly where they need to correct their thinking. We are *all* the same. We are *all* significant. We are *all* important.

Remember, there is no one who is any bit more blessed than another. No one who is any bit more worthy of the angels than any other.

We are all important! We are all worthy. And the seemingly insignificant minutiae of our lives are equally important.

Why? Because they are important to us. Because they make up the substance of our present-moment experience. And because they are our starting point from which we can emerge onto the path of awakening.

Some of you may shrink from this notion of such intimate and direct contact with the angelic realm. If you can speak to the emissaries of God, the emissaries of your own unique divine wisdom, then what will you do with this wisdom they might afford you? Will you have the courage and the faith to truly embrace their guidance?

It is one thing to seek guidance and knowledge, but what then? What will you do with it? What responsibility do you undertake when you know better, when you have been guided, when that which was unclear is made more clear?

When you step upon this path of discovery and seek guidance from the heavens, Truth becomes either your best friend or possibly your greatest enemy. For the revelation of truth can set you free if you have the courage and the faith to look within and grow.

Or your resistance to facing truth will cause your life to become even more chaotic, uncomfortable, sad, frustrating and painful. Because this will be life's way of telling you to get off the fence, to examine yourself and your life more honestly and to choose differently!

After all, it is really not that difficult. Ultimately what are we choosing for? We are simply choosing for whatever it is that we can grasp in the moment as that which expands our loving experience of ourselves, of others and of life itself.

So many people are living unhappy, unfulfilled lives. So many are on paths which do not bring them any depth or any meaning. They are just living their lives day to day and doing their best to survive, often even unwilling to acknowledge their emptiness.

And in order to validate their numbing experiences, they adopt beliefs which support their suffering. Beliefs that ennoble their suffering and declare it to be an integral part of the path to God.

In truth, this is not so. Suffering is only the experience of one who has not expanded into his divinity. Suffering is the experience of one who denies the brilliant divinity of his life. Suffering is the experience of one who has not yet found the courage to see that his life is his own creation.

It is simpler to relegate the cause of your sadness, your misery, your fatigue, and your frustration to others or to God. Some even call it a punishment from God. Some even claim that this punishment is a *gift* from God—that He uses to test only the dearest of souls.

I say, it is far easier for them to adopt these projections rather than to look within for the cause of their malaise.

And why do they resist the inner search? Because they believe deep within that to examine themselves is to judge themselves. And judgment is a broad sword, lethal with its damning power.

I remind you here again. Judgment is not real. It is merely a human construct, something designed by unwise souls who themselves could not look upon their own lives with compassion and mercy. For if they had done so, they would have seen that there is truly nothing to judge. Everything that has been, everything that *ever* has been, is simply experience. And experience is wisdom-gained.

To embrace this understanding is at once to see this truth in yourself and to see it in all others. And this will result in only one conclusion: we are all the same.

It is the time now in the evolution of humanity and our planet to examine ourselves and our lives. It is time to be honest. It is time to forego complacency and to stop pretending that everything is fine.

For do you not think that God and the angels and your spirit guides know the truth? They do! And they have no judgment! Only compassion.

Do not compromise! Who are you to compromise yourself? You are divine! Do you not yet see yourself that way?

Claim your power! Claim your truth! Claim your brilliance! And make earth-shattering choices that define you in this new light.

For remember that when we do meet I will be asking you,

*Who are you to say you are not Divine?*

## The Ninth Moon

*The ninth moon was rising as I sighed.*

*It was a sigh of reflection,*
*A pause*
*To look upon the days and the nights*
*Since my first moon in this magical place.*

*And as she sailed above illuminating my heart,*
*I recounted my joys and my riches...*

*Lovers, family, friends—my greatest of treasures.*

*On this night, the moon's gentle arc lit a liquid path*
*Across the sea and over the world's edge.*

*It was to the other side that she was going.*
*And it is to this other side that I would follow.*

*What softness will she reveal to me there?*

# ABOUT THE AUTHOR

Shams-Tabriz was born in Kampala, Uganda and emigrated as a young child with his family to Canada. A seasoned entrepreneur, Shams-Tabriz has been successful in such diverse sectors as food processing and real estate development. First a student in Montreal, Shams-Tabriz later pursued Near Eastern Studies and Economics in Seattle. He then honed himself in the workplace, discovering a passion for innovation, team-building and problem-solving.

As the founder of The Rumi Group—a visionary body with plans for next-level socially responsible ventures—Shams-Tabriz aims to extend the socio-economic benefits of successful markets to producers in the world's poorest regions, where people often have raw desire, resources and skills yet lack access to training, capital and markets to improve their livelihood. The core impulse behind the establishment of The Rumi Group is the hope that the forces of compassion and unity may awaken a sense of interdependence and universal harmony that will lead to the betterment of the lives of humanity at large.

Shams-Tabriz also serves as a director of Open To Grow, a charitable organization providing training and microfinance to grassroots women workers in Central America.

The stories told in this book capture the highlights of Shams-Tabriz's ongoing spiritual adventure.

*Soaring With Angels, The Workshop Series* is another project of Shams-Tabriz which aims to expand the understanding and impact of the facets of divine discovery for all who are so compelled to step fully onto their own paths to brilliance.

Visit *www.soaringwithangels.com* for more.

Made in the USA
Charleston, SC
03 April 2012